"AUTHORITATIVE READING ON A SUBJECT OF
PERPETUAL INTEREST" —*Booklist*

Today's world is one w   have
rewritten old rules abou   nent
with a firm. Yet it's also a world where virtues like loyalty,
honesty, and hard work are still keys to advancement. It's
a world where how you dress, how you write the English
language, how you behave, how you treat others both
above and below you in an organization, vitally affect
how far up the ladder you go. It's a world where little
things can make huge differences—and where Robert Half
can show you what to look for, what to do, what to avoid.
This extraordinary guide offers up-to-date advice and creative approaches to finding that better job in today's "crazy"
new employment strategy.

HOW TO GET A BETTER JOB
IN THIS CRAZY WORLD

"As chairman of the board, I'm not looking for a different
job. But if I were, this would be my guidebook."
                    —William A. Schreyer, Chairman and CEO,
                        Merrill Lynch & Co., Inc.

ROBERT HALF is a frequent guest on network television
and radio, writes monthly columns, including one in the
National Business Employment Weekly, and has previously
published five books, including *Robert Half on Hiring*
(available in a Plume edition). Mr. Half resides in Florida.

BOOKS BY ROBERT HALF

The Robert Half Way to Get Hired in Today's Job Market

Robert Half's Success Guide for Accountants

Robert Half on Hiring

Making It Big in Data Processing

How to Get a Better Job in This Crazy World

HOW TO GET A BETTER JOB IN THIS CRAZY WORLD

Robert Half

A PLUME BOOK

PLUME
Published by the Penguin Group
Penguin Books USA Inc., 375 Hudson Street, New York, New York 10014, U.S.A.
Penguin Books Ltd, 27 Wrights Lane, London W8 5TZ, England
Penguin Books Australia Ltd, Ringwood, Victoria, Australia
Penguin Books Canada Ltd, 2801 John Street, Markham, Ontario, Canada L3R 1B4
Penguin Books (N.Z.) Ltd, 182–190 Wairau Road, Auckland 10, New Zealand

Penguin Books Ltd, Registered Offices: Harmondsworth, Middlesex, England

Published by Plume, an imprint of New American Library, a division of Penguin Books
USA Inc. This is an authorized reprint of a hardcover edition published by Crown
Publishers, Inc.

First Plume Printing, April, 1991
10 9 8 7 6 5 4 3 2 1

 REGISTERED TRADEMARK—MARCA REGISTRADA

Half, Robert.
    How to get a better job in this crazy world / Robert Half.
      p.   cm.
    Reprint. Originally published: New York : Crown, c1990.
    ISBN 0-517-57346-6
    1. Job hunting.   I. Title.
  [HF5382.7.H33   1990b]
  650.14—dc20
                                          90–7904
                                            CIP

Printed in the United States of America
Original hardcover design by Shari deMiskey

And they shall be among those
who will inherit this crazy world
—hopefully for the better.

Stephanie
Kevin
Ryan
Adam

CONTENTS

ACKNOWLEDGMENTS

Help helps

Help is what you get when you ask for it,
and sometimes when you don't.

I appreciate the help and support of my good friend
Harold M. Messmer, Jr., Chairman and CEO of Robert
Half International Inc.; and its excellent management
team of Max Thelen III, Robert W. Glass, and Keith
Waddell.

And to my friend Don Bain, whose encouragement and
advice were helpful; to James O. Wade, my astute and
understanding editor; and to my wife, Maxine, who
tolerated this whole thing.

READ THIS FIRST

IF I'D BEEN TOLD FORTY YEARS AGO BY A FOR-
tune-teller that men and women in the 1990s would be
tested for drugs; be advised to learn Japanese to enhance
their careers; be prohibited from smoking on the job; successfully sue former employers for having been fired or
given a bad reference; choose their doctors and lawyers
from newspaper ads; go to jail for misusing insider information; fail to advance because of a lack of basic computer skills; have children through surrogate mothers;
choose from hundreds of TV channels; donate their eyes
and hearts to organ banks (or receive organs from them);
jog twelve miles a day, stopping only to grab a bite at any
one of three dozen fast-food outlets in their neighborhood; find their garbage taking extended cruises in search
of a dumping site; have their memos transmitted instan-
taneously all over the world via fax machines; routinely
make telephone calls from their cars; be afraid to walk
the streets; and have a president of the United States who
consults an astrologer...I would have said, "The world
can't become *that* crazy."

But it *has* become that crazy when viewed from a
certain perspective. Vast societal changes have dramati-

1

cally altered every aspect of the way we live and conduct business—sometimes for the better. If you need proof, simply consider the women's movement, which has changed the way many homes and businesses function.

A readership poll conducted by London's prestigious *Economist* identifies the women's movement as the most important change in society over the past hundred years. Obviously, the women's movement is anything but "crazy." Much good has come out of it. Women are now free to explore other avenues of self-fulfillment beyond motherhood; a pay-equalizing trend for men and women has been put into motion; a wide range of occupational opportunities has opened; a previous second-class-citizen status for women is no longer acceptable; and the female perspective has contributed substantially to business success and to a wide variety of governmental affairs.

Still, it has changed our society to the extent that we risk *going* crazy trying to understand it and keep up with it.

At the same time, we've created a greenhouse effect that threatens life on our planet; long-distance bus and train travel has virtually disappeared; we toss out a piece of sophisticated electronic equipment when it needs to be repaired because it's cheaper to buy a new one; state governments have become bookies through off-track betting and lotteries; crime may be our biggest business, and growing rapidly; over one-third of our population is functionally illiterate; our students demonstrate an appalling lack of knowledge of such basics as international and domestic geography, history, reading, writing, math, and economics (whole generations have received their basic information through TV, which, by its very nature, almost never provides in-depth understanding of major issues); and, while all this goes on, foreign companies are engaged in a steady, successful program of buying up America.

Obviously, many changes that contribute to a world perceived as being somewhat crazy have brought about positive opportunities, too. We have more options in our professional and personal lives than ever before, including international business possibilities helped, to a great extent, by such new technologies as instant global communication. A greater sense of equality has evolved, and diverse approaches to old problems are more appreciated. American managers have been challenged to do a better job. The hiring field is now characterized by a substantially greater emphasis on fairness than when I started my business more than forty years ago.

Not too long ago, a placement counselor working for me referred a highly qualified candidate to an employer looking for precisely this individual's skills and experience. That candidate was turned down because he was overweight. ("Fat people steal," the employer explained.) What could my counselor do except shake her head and say, "It's a crazy world."

"What a crazy world" was the only thing left to say when another employer turned down an excellent job candidate because, when asked whether she'd ever been given a speeding ticket, she answered truthfully by saying no. (The employer reasoned that anyone who hadn't been given a speeding ticket moved too slowly for his business.)

What's left to say when employers hire by astrological signs?

Or when a job candidate turns down a lucrative job offer because the employer refuses to pay for his wife's ballet lessons and to transport his boat from Australia to Chicago? "It's a crazy world out there."

When corporate restructuring results in widespread layoffs and causes employees no longer to display loyalty to their employers...when the insatiable greed of bright, talented, and educated young people puts them behind bars...when Little League teams and Boy Scout troops have to close down because the cost of buying liability insurance is too great...when these and myriad other things occur, all that's left to do is toss up our hands and say, "It's a crazy world."

The problem for those who opt to toss up their hands in surrender is that, while such an action might provide momentary psychological relief, it won't result in landing that better job. For job seekers, and career builders, there are two clear choices:

1. Change the world.

2. Figure out how to get a better job in the world as it exists.

Obviously, each of us should attempt to make this world a little saner, but we can't postpone looking for that better job until the world has changed to our specifications (it's amazing how many people take this approach). Our lives aren't dress rehearsals; this is it, and the degree of success we achieve in our chosen professions and occupations will directly result from how we go about building our careers—how we go about finding a better job in this real world, crazy or not.

I've written this book for the millions of men and women who, with dedication, hard work, and good advice, will find better jobs. Naturally, each person has his or her own definition of what constitutes a better job. For some, a better job means increased security. For others, it's represented by greater challenge and the opportunity to prosper from successful risk taking. For still others, more money equates with having found a better job. It doesn't matter how you define it; the important thing is to make the most of what you have, to reach rather than to settle, to analyze the world in which you must function, and to take whatever steps are necessary to achieve your personal goals.

I know this book will help.

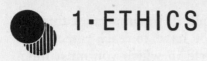

1·ETHICS

That quaint, all-but-forgotten, but slowly
returning concept called *ethics*

> *No one is more ethical than someone who*
> *has just become ethical.*

FOR SOMEONE SEEKING A BETTER JOB IN TODAY'S
world, the word *ethics* could be the most important word
in your vocabulary, rivaled only, perhaps, by *loyalty*.

Whatever happened to ethics?

There was a time when most people naturally dealt
from an ethical base in their personal and business lives.
There were, of course, exceptions, but they were just that
—exceptions, not the rule. Ethical conduct wasn't something that one studied in school. We were brought up to
be ethical. Those who delve into the subject of ethics are
called *deontologists*. They've been writing about ethical
behavior for centuries, and those individuals who lived
blatantly unethical lives in years gone by were usually
viewed with understandable scorn.

Then things began to change. I won't attempt to analyze why this change occurred. I leave that to the deontologists. I do know that society did a flip-flop; unethical
behavior seems to have become more common, and those

who insisted upon acting in an ethical manner evoked
snickers from their less ethical colleagues, who equated
ethics with unabashed patriotism, loyalty to friends and
employers, and a belief in the tooth fairy. In 1893 Thomas
Huxley wrote *Evolution and Ethics*, in which he called for
a constant reevaluation of every step of mankind's progress in search of "the ethical process." Lately his sage advice has frequently been ignored.

In the workplace unethical behavior is basically
practiced in two ways and by two distinct groups of people, and the differentiation should be made.

Workers, particularly those who represent what came
to be known as the "Me Generation," are unethical when
they fail to work hard, to honestly account for their time
and expenses, and when they steal an employer's time.
They are clearly unethical when they reveal trade secrets
to competitors, and when they create résumés that do not
honestly represent their background and skills. For them
—and their impact upon the American economic base in
the fiercely competitive global economy has been substantial, not to say destructive—ethics can best be defined by the term *work ethic* or, in this case, a lack of it.
Certain values expressed by the Me Generation were positive, at least at the time of their inception. There was a
focus upon personal values rather than business success.
While on the surface that rings of a worthwhile human
commitment, it often carried into the workplace the lack
of dedication that was at odds with the needs of business.

It is a mistake, however, to view the ramifications of
the Me Generation's approach as being represented only
by employees. Employers—the other side of the ethical
coin—often practice unethical business behavior because
of unabashed greed and a lack of social responsibility.
There is no question in my mind that many corporate
cultures are as much a part of the Me Generation as are

the individuals who work for them. The fact is that an employer's pattern of doing business will often affect the conduct of employees throughout their work lives, for better or for worse.

For the ethical man or woman seeking a better job, this sometimes depressing situation offers a golden opportunity.

I've heard hundreds, perhaps thousands of employers say, "I'm not looking for anything unusual when I hire people. All I want are employees who will do what they're supposed to do." It's my judgment, however, that an employee who doesn't do what he or she is supposed to—assuming there is more than adequate guidance—is either not qualified for the job or unethical.

For a number of years now our organization has conducted, through an independent research company, an annual survey of how much time is stolen by American workers. The theft of an employer's time occurs when long and unnecessary personal calls are made on a company phone, when workers linger over coffee or at the water cooler (the copying machine has largely taken its place), when they deliberately drag their feet on a project, and in all the other everyday situations that have become much too common in American offices and factories. The numbers are staggering; our 1988 study indicated that $200 billion worth of employee time was stolen that year from American employers. It is the Me Generation at its worst.

Employee theft certainly isn't limited to time. It's estimated that American employees steal more than $4 billion a year in cash and merchandise. Employee theft of tangible assets costs management about $1.50 per worker per day. Sadly, some managers view employee theft as part of the cost of doing business. In one extreme case, a manager monitored how much each employee stole each year, and so long as the dollar amount didn't exceed how much each person in the company was being underpaid, he accepted it.

Managers of American business are certainly not blind to any of this, although their collective lack of corrective action could easily lead an observer to conclude that they have been, at best, wearing blinders. As these managers and those to follow see their competitive position erode, they must come to the obvious conclusion that low productivity and the outright theft of both goods and time are factors in this slippage.

As business has recognized its ethical failings, and as the business community has confronted the difficult ethical choices resulting from an increasingly complex world, business leaders have taken certain corrective measures.

Ethics is now taught in business schools.

Ethics is now taught within corporations.

The corporate motto of Robert Half International is "Ethics First." Of course, the employment services industry was characterized early on by too many unethical individuals and firms. (There are still a few around, but the number has, fortunately, dwindled.) Most of the ones that function on an ethical base have survived and prospered. Most of those that didn't are gone.

Have we become a nation of liars? A *U.S. News & World Report*–CNN poll found that more than half the people in the survey feel we're less honest than a decade ago. A House subcommittee estimated that one out of three working Americans was hired after submitting falsified or deceptive credentials (which matches up with our own studies). A 1987 study accused forty-seven leading scientists at Harvard and Emory University medical schools of producing "misleading" papers.

An ethical and honest man or woman seeking a better

job in this crazy world is at a premium and stands an increasing chance of being rewarded.

How can ethical people seeking a better job indicate that they bring this precious attribute of ethics to a prospective employer, along with their education, experience, and skills?

It begins with the résumé and cover letter sent to a personnel recruiter or a company. Our research over the years indicates that more than 30 percent of all job seekers lie on their résumés, which doesn't include lies of omission. Because so many job seekers have adopted this dishonest approach, and so many companies have been stung by bogus credentials and work histories, employers are beginning to get tougher and more methodical in checking references.

A whole new industry has sprung up whose sole purpose is to check the background of job candidates. Companies that provide psychological and drug testing are thriving, and new laws have been enacted in response to these efforts to test employees.

Be honest on your résumé and in the letters you write. This doesn't mean focusing on negative aspects of your background, but it *does* mean that you should not claim jobs and responsibilities you didn't have. It means being honest about your education. It means being direct in the language you use, rather than skirting the truth. Increasingly, résumé "puffing" is being detected by skilled personnel directors and corporate executives.

Go after a better job with the attitude that you would rather lose a job opportunity than gain one based upon deceit. Put your best foot forward, of course, but don't say things that could cause you embarrassment and, by extension, the loss of a good opportunity that you might have won without the falsehoods. Be eager, interested in opportunity and growth, and open to varied job potentials.

Before seeking a better job in this too often unethical world, define for yourself your own ethical standards, and be ready to express them when asked during an interview. The first step here is to be honest in evaluating your view of ethics. A sound set of ethics isn't mysterious, and doesn't need a grounding in ancient philosophy to develop in any of us. Ethical behavior is based upon common tenets of fairness, decency, and an adherence to the spirit and letter of the law. By conducting yourself in business in accord with those precepts, you may suffer the scornful smile of a less ethical person. On the other hand, you'll have positioned yourself as someone who can be trusted, which, I assure you, will stand you in good stead when seeking a better job.

You see, what has happened is what invariably happens to all swings in a society. The pendulum reaches its extremity (the point at which a majority of people realize that the old way causes more harm than good and no longer works) and begins its slow swing back. I truly believe that our recent lack of ethical behavior has resulted in enough damage to our national base, to companies, and to individuals to force the pendulum to begin its return to an ethical center. That means that job seekers who've anticipated that trend, and react accordingly by developing a commitment to ethics, will be ahead of the pack.

Hopefully, this will put an end to job candidates' telling trade secrets to their present company's competitors in order to impress a prospective new employer. It was always a source of wonderment to me that any potential employer would be impressed by this approach, but it *is* a crazy world. Ethical employees don't do this, which means *you* shouldn't as you seek a better job.

An ethical employee doesn't steal an employer's time by making frequent and lengthy personal phone calls during office hours, or by using the photocopying machine and fax machine for personal business without permission.

An ethical person does not discuss sensitive company business with inappropriate people, which, of course, includes someone with whom you're interviewing for a better job. If you'll do it with that person, any realistic and sensible employer will assume you would do the same thing about his or her company. Discretion is a flattering and appealing trait in everyone, especially when seeking a better job.

An ethical person in the business world abides by a company's rules, even if they don't match up with the individual's wishes. Conveying respect for your present employer's rules to a prospective new employer is impressive.

Ethical behavior extends to how you leave a job. I get into this subject in depth in a subsequent chapter. For now, keep in mind that when a new employer asks, "When can you start?" the ethical response is "I think I owe my present employer a decent amount of time to find my replacement," rather than "I can be here tomorrow." Of course, if you're unemployed, by all means say "tomorrow."

Like tennis, ethics benefits from careful thought and practice.

Practice ethics as you seek a better job, and while you're at it, sharpen up your sense of *loyalty*, too.

Reminders About Ethics

≡ Don't be a time thief.

≡ Thirty percent of job seekers lie on their résumés. Don't lie on yours.

■ Be honest, but focus on your strengths rather than your weaknesses.

■ Not getting a job is better than getting one deceitfully.

■ Don't divulge your present employer's trade secrets to a prospective new employer. It doesn't impress anyone.

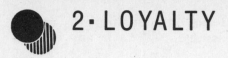

2·LOYALTY

Loyalty is a two-way street

LIKE BUSINESS ETHICS, COMPANY AND EMPLOYEE loyalty has declined somewhere along the way. In many ways it was inevitable, and at times has been justified. Loyalty can work only when the street is two-way. As companies are being gobbled up, then carved up, and we don't know who the boss is any longer—to say nothing of companies trying to meet foreign competition by getting "lean and mean,"—many good and loyal employees at all levels are finding themselves unemployed. Companies are demanding loyalty from their employees, yet giving little of it in return. The psychological contract between many employers and employees no longer exists.

Consider this: of the one hundred largest companies in 1917, only eleven were left in 1987. Actually, another eleven survived, but under a different name. Even including them, the dropout rate is 78 percent.

That loyalty pendulum, like the ethics one, although perhaps not beginning its swing in the opposite direction as yet, is close to reaching its own maximum arc. It will take a new breed of manager to start it in a direction characterized by a sense of loyalty that cuts both ways. That new manager could be you, along with millions of

14

others who progress into positions of authority. As the managerial ranks begin to swell with men and women who approach their own careers with a renewed sense of loyalty, their attitude will become company policy, turning today's one-way street into one with two lanes. It will happen. Too many companies and individuals have been hurt by a lack of loyalty and will begin demanding it again—from both directions.

The generation of the forties placed career and family above personal fulfillment. The Me Generation of the seventies and eighties preached loyalty to yourself above all else. Like many ideas, these were taken too far by extremists. There is a fair and sensible middle ground upon which loyalty in the workplace should and will be established again.

Yes, we must be "loyal" to ourselves. If you find yourself in a work situation in which you're being unfairly treated, underpaid, abused, or stymied in your career climb, you owe it to yourself to look elsewhere. Leaving a job for something better isn't an act of disloyalty. But so long as you accept a salary from an employer, you owe that company your best efforts. You owe it the courtesy of not bad-mouthing it to others, particularly competitors. And if you *really* want to be loyal to yourself in your quest for a better job, don't automatically assume that you must look elsewhere. That's something else that this crazy world has fostered, a belief that job hopping is the only route to success. Headhunters have no problem recruiting these days. Employment industry surveys claim that more than 90 percent of executives return calls to headhunters. The figure was 80 percent ten years ago and only 50 percent twenty years ago. People now quit good jobs at the drop of an offer.

Years ago, someone who often changed jobs was viewed with suspicion. Yet, even in today's chaotic workplace, years of hard work with one company pay off. The majority of corporate presidents and CEOs have been with their companies for ten years or more.

Losing employees and having to replace them is costly and time-consuming. Estimates vary, but there is a general consensus that it costs a company about one and a half times an employee's annual salary to hire and train a replacement. And, of course, replacing an employee means lower productivity for a period of time, and an unsettling effect upon all others in the department.

Companies are realizing this with increasing regularity and are going back to rewarding good employees. Again, this takes a change in attitude on both sides—management and employee. It's beginning to happen, albeit slowly, because it has to happen, and men and women who approach the search for a better job with ethics and loyalty as part of their basic attitude stand a better chance than ever of being rewarded over the long haul.

Someone looking for a new and better job instantly displays a lack of good judgment and discretion when telling an interviewer how mismanaged, unpleasant, and generally fouled up his or her current company is. The same image is conveyed when rapping your present boss. Don't, no matter how justified you might feel such comments are. The interviewer may seem interested, might even give the impression of enjoying what you're saying about your employer, but knows that you'll end up saying similar things about him or her.

The longer you work in a field, the smaller that field becomes. We each establish an image of ourselves with employers and co-workers, and that image is hard to change. It travels with us as we seek greater opportunity and better jobs. The person you work next to today may well end up being in a position to hire you five years from now. Present to that person every day an image of a loyal and ethical person. *That's* an image you'll never have to think about changing.

Respect your employer's time and money. If your company doesn't prosper in this competitive world, neither will you. Avoid the game that became popular over the past couple of decades, the one in which you go out and make as much as you can for doing as little as possible. Do more than you have to do to just get by.

There has been an interesting shift in attitudes toward work lately, one that everyone seeking a better job should take note of. Back in the 1950s, when the economy was booming, housing was plentiful and cheap, and jobs were easily available, the work ethic that characterized that period of prosperity started to be questioned. There was a growing emphasis on leisure time. It wasn't a negative thing; it didn't represent a generation lazier than the previous one. In fact, it was perceived by many as the first opportunity for this nation to move into a classical "golden age." A special issue of *Life* magazine focused on this, the writers proclaiming that America was about to become "freer and bolder than the Greeks, more just and powerful than the Romans, wiser than the Confucian, saner than the French, more responsible than the Victorian, and happier than all of them together."

The idea was that as more Americans became prosperous, they would enjoy more free time and use it for the betterment of society.

That was a nice concept, but it didn't work.

Many things caused the eventual disillusionment with it, primarily the reality of our corporate society as we entered the 1980s. Many of those who had become successful and prosperous not only were uncomfortable with an excess of leisure time, they found it impossible to indulge in it because of economic reality. As some of the well-to-do returned to the workplace with a vengeance, an unfortunate attitude developed among average workers that was a harbinger of the Me Generation to come. A survey in 1968 showed that 58 percent of the people interviewed felt that hard work truly paid off. The same survey done in 1983 indicated that only 36 percent felt that way. I believe that if the survey were taken now, the percentage of those subscribing to hard work would be close to the 1968 figure. Hard work has always paid off, and always will. The fact that those who don't need to work hard are working harder than ever is a good indication of this.

Why do these people work as hard as they do?

It's obvious to me that they have a tremendous pride in their daily business lives and are committed to seeing things done right, even if that means long hours and extra effort.

Speaking from personal experience, even after selling my own company, I find myself devoting as much time—perhaps in some ways more—to the aspects of the business with which I'm involved on a continuing basis. I still enjoy the work, and find the long hours and intense effort satisfying rather than a hardship. I find that work is never work when you enjoy what you're doing—it's fun, and most people can always find time to have fun.

I always advice young people to give themselves a chance to enjoy the challenge of a hard day's work. It's a good feeling, one that is being increasingly appreciated by a growing number of men and women now seeking better jobs. The demand for instant gratification that has characterized many of our bright and educated people will, unless abandoned, keep them from achieving the level of success to which they aspire.

Ethical, loyal employees are the last to be let go when a company runs into difficulty. It makes sense, just as hiring someone with a reputation for being ethical and loyal makes sense. In a climate in which those traits are

not especially plentiful, those who possess and practice
them stand a significantly better chance of getting a better job in this frequently crazy, unethical, disloyal world.

Reminders on Loyalty

☰ The psychological contract between employer
and employee no longer exists.

☰ Be loyal to yourself. Looking for a new and better
job does not indicate a lack of loyalty to your
present employer.

☰ Don't bad-mouth anyone.

☰ Loyal employees and loyal employers are about
to become a precious commodity once again.

☰ The longer you work in a field, the smaller that
field becomes. Be nice to everyone, and be known
as a loyal and ethical person.

☰ Respect your employer's time and money. If your
company doesn't prosper, neither will you.

☰ Commit yourself to the sort of work ethic that
has been lost in the past few decades.

☰ Men and women known as loyal, ethical individuals get hired faster and are the last to be let go.

3 · ETIQUETTE

Manners maketh the man (and the woman)

LOYALTY AND ETHICS ARE NOT THE ONLY THINGS lacking in today's world and workplace. Etiquette has become a confusing topic in the workplace. It needn't be. Etiquette is, after all, nothing more than showing consideration to others in every type of human interchange. Unfortunately, too many people seem oblivious to its importance.

The reasons for this are fairly obvious. We've passed through the period of "do your own thing" which, by its very definition, abandons the need—to say nothing of the motivation—to worry about how we treat our fellow human beings. When self-centeredness rules in our personal lives, it causes anger and resentment in others. When it predominates in business, it can result in the loss of clients, lower morale, and declining productivity and competitiveness in any enterprise. The self-centered or narcissistic individual will probably fail to get that better job for which he or she is looking.

It always saddens me to see bright and highly educated young men and women fumble through interviews, either in the employer's office or over a meal, because they are unsure of what good etiquette is all about. These people don't necessarily do anything wrong, but they are unable to project confidence because they're worrying about rules of etiquette they never bothered to learn.

An analogy can be made to someone who has to give a speech. The speaker goes to the podium with something wrong with his or her clothing—a button dangling by a thread, or a stain on a shirt or blouse. The dangling button or stain is always on the speaker's mind, which, of course, means that some of the focus on the speech itself is lost. Job seekers should take great pains to make sure that when they go for an interview their clothing is clean and pressed and is appropriate to the job they're seeking. And, while making sure your appearance is without flaws, you should go into this sort of important interchange between you and an employer fully aware of what good etiquette requires in one's behavior.

Of course we're speaking here of basic manners, accepted protocol, common sense. Then there are those job seekers who go into an interview and don't simply make mistakes in etiquette—they rewrite the book.

A few years ago, while I was writing *Robert Half on Hiring*, I commissioned a survey of top executives and personnel managers in which I asked, "What was the most unusual thing that a job candidate ever did at an interview?" They reported many unusual incidents, but here are a few that especially caught my attention.

≡ "He wouldn't leave unless I offered him a job. I had to call the police."

≡ "She told me to put on my suit jacket to make the atmosphere more formal."

≡ "He pulled out a Polaroid camera and took my picture. He said he always takes a picture of everybody who interviews him."

≡ "I took a phone call. The candidate took out a box of Kentucky Fried Chicken, put it on my desk, and started eating."

≡ "I asked him about his hobbies. He jumped up and started tap dancing."

≡ "She told me that if I didn't hire her, she'd have her grandmother put a curse on me."

≡ "Jumped up and down on my carpet and said I must be a big shot to have such thick carpeting."

Bizarre, of course, but only because these people acted in an extreme way. Many of the responses to the survey pointed to simple bad manners that left a negative image in the interviewer's mind: sloppy eating habits, unpleasant personal habits, interrupting a conversation— ordinary examples of bad etiquette that we see far too much of these days.

If you aren't sure of what good etiquette is all about, get a book out of the library and learn. Even if you think you're pretty well versed in etiquette, you can avoid potentially awkward situations by thinking ahead. If you're going to be interviewed over lunch or dinner, remind yourself not to order anything that is difficult to eat, like spaghetti, or dishes that are messy and demand the use of fingers, like lobster. Obviously, avoid items from the menu that are heavy on garlic or onions.

I remember a story about a young man who was being interviewed for a job over lunch. His potential boss ordered steak tartare. The young man had no idea what steak tartare was, but decided to order it, telling the waiter, "Make mine well done." The moral is to avoid not only dishes that are difficult to eat but those you can't pronounce or know nothing about.

Even though some other dishes on the menu may appeal to you, your purpose is not to have a good meal. You're there to smoothly progress through the lunch or dinner without butchering the foreign name of a dish or struggling with food that could end up in your lap.

Do not drink *any* alcoholic beverages during a business interview. Even a glass of wine can dull your senses; a job interview is when you need to be at your sharpest. If your prospective employer has a drink, pass anyway. You don't have to create the impression that you never drink; a simple "Not right now, thank you" indicates that you're not averse to drinking but don't choose to at the moment. This has become increasingly important because of the changed attitude toward drinking. The day of the three-martini lunch is long gone. I commissioned a study in which top executives were asked what percentage of today's executives consume alcoholic beverages during a typical business lunch. In their opinion, only 26 percent did, compared to their estimate of 37 percent five years ago—a whopping 30 percent decrease.

If you haven't quit smoking yet, stifle the urge until you're far away from your potential new boss. The best advice is to quit smoking altogether. Not only will your chances of a long life increase, your potential for career success will be significantly enhanced. I've commissioned numerous studies on smoking in the workplace, and the results are clear-cut and significant. In another survey of top executives, we found that only 22 percent of the men and women running our top corporations smoke (61 percent of them used to smoke). When asked to estimate the percentage of smokers in their firms, they responded that 14 percent of top management smokes, 19 percent of middle management, and 24 percent of staff personnel. I read that as indicating that there's some correlation between smoking and job success. Smokers clearly darken their chances of rising to top management or, in an increasing number of cases, getting employed at all.

Another smoking study, perhaps even more relevant for the readers of this book who are seeking better jobs, asked executives: "If you had to choose between two job candidates, each equally qualified to do the job, but one a smoker and one not, which would you choose?" These executives chose the nonsmoker by a ratio of fifteen to one. Clearly, smoking can be hazardous to your wealth.

Don't bring someone with you to an interview. That creates an awkward situation for everyone concerned. The receptionist has to pay attention to a person whose presence has no practical meaning to the business going on, and you sit during the interview wondering whether your companion is getting bored sitting in the waiting room. It just isn't good business etiquette. If you must have someone accompany you, have him or her wait for you at a place totally removed from the building in which the interview is taking place.

When interviewed in an office, politely decline an offer of coffee or something to eat. It just puts you in a position of possibly spilling the coffee, dropping crumbs on the executive's rug, or having a mouth filled with pastry just as you're asked "Where do you want to be ten years from now?"

Being on time to all appointments is good etiquette. Being late to any appointment is not. One of my surveys showed that 93 percent of key hiring decision makers felt that candidates who arrive late for job interviews take a giant step toward remaining unemployed.

Leave for an interview with plenty of time to spare, even if you have to kill a half hour in a local coffee shop. Arriving early gives you a chance to make sure you can find the address and the proper floor, and precludes your coming into the interview breathless and disorganized.

For the same reason, bring a minimum of materials with you. If it's a rainy day, politely ask the receptionist or secretary whether you can leave your umbrella and rain-coat outside the interview room. The more you carry into an interview, the more you will have to juggle. Be prepared to shake hands; having to shift things from one arm to the other while the interviewer stands there with his or her hand dangling in midair is not very impressive.

Speaking of handshakes, be sure yours is firm. Don't overdo it, however. There is a whole world of men who equate a firm handshake with crunching the knuckles of another man. To say the least, this can cause the wrong kind of lasting impression.

We've all heard how important direct eye contact is. That's true, but there are individuals who are so obsessed with this need that they spend an entire interview staring intently into the eyes of the interviewer, which is guaranteed to create tension. Eye contact can be accomplished by directing your gaze at the forehead or nose. I'm not suggesting avoiding the eyes, but don't feel that you have to lock in like a laser beam from the minute you sit down.

More thank-you notes never get written because people are unsure of their ability to put something in writing and so don't. Then again, many people have never been taught that proper etiquette demands thanking someone beyond the perfunctory "Thanks" when leaving an interview. A thank-you note need be only a few lines, but be certain to add something to it that will enhance your image—maybe one of your strong points that did not come out during the interview: "Thank you very much for your time and courtesy yesterday. I'm pleased to be considered for the job, and am even more enthusiastic about the possibility now that we've met. By the way, I didn't mention yesterday that the computer program I helped to create with XYZ Corp. resulted in a 26 percent savings the first year. Again, thank you. Sincerely, ..."

There is a legion of people who practice proper business etiquette only with those they deem worthy of it by virtue of position or title. This is a serious mistake, and I wouldn't even want to guess how many otherwise qualified job candidates lose the job before they even arrive for the interview. Every person with whom you come in contact should be considered extremely important and worthy of your best etiquette. I remember on a few occasions having my secretary call in to me and say quietly, "Mr. Half, there's a very rude man out here who has an appointment with you." Those few words ensured that this candidate would not get the job I was looking to fill.

Now that better jobs in the workplace are no longer a male monopoly, there is a great deal of natural confusion about the "new rules" of etiquette between men and women working side by side. While this confusion is a natural outgrowth of a shift in the role of women in society, it needn't be as stressful as many people make it.

The best approach, I think, is for a man to naturally practice the sort of courtesy toward women that he was taught and grew up with (assuming, of course, that he *was* taught the proper etiquette with the opposite sex). When a man meets a female colleague for the first time, by all means he should reach to open a door through which the two of them will pass. If she accepts this gesture graciously, the man should make a mental note that with this particular woman it's all right to open the door for her. The same applies to standing when she enters your office, or helping to remove her coat.

If you are a woman, you can minimize confusion and social awkwardness by having a clear sense of the extent to which you will accept male courtesies in the workplace. If a man reaches to open the door and you prefer to open doors yourself, you should pleasantly say, "Thanks,

I've got it." An astute male will note this, and the next time the two of you are about to go through a door, there will be no confusion.

These suggestions apply with colleagues with whom you work regularly. Obviously, if you're a man about to be interviewed for a job by a woman executive, and she personally escorts you to her office from the reception area, it would be inappropriate for you to open her office door. In this situation—as in virtually every other basic common courtesy practiced between any two human beings —behavior should be appropriate and prudent.

Avoiding confusion in today's workplace demands sensitivity on the part of both men and women. Women who loudly crusade against any sign of male deference to them in such simple matters as opening doors or helping remove coats create tensions that are unnecessary. By the same token, men who are insensitive to the changing needs of the workplace only limit their chances of success. They end up offending their female colleagues.

Some men consider the gains made by women in the workplace "silly" and see having to change their chauvinistic views of women as an unnecessary intrusion into their lives. Men who carry that view into American business today are virtually guaranteed to find their advancement stymied. Women working alongside such men resent being called "sweetie" and "honey." Like it or not, the workplace is now and shall forever be a place of gender neutrality. Understand and respect that fact and the etiquette that goes with it. Those men who don't will have to settle for less in their careers.

So many rules of good business etiquette seem obvious, yet are broken every day. If, during an interview, the interviewer mispronounces a word, control the urge to pronounce it correctly. Better to avoid using it for the rest of the interview. Don't criticize the restaurant you've been taken to for the interview. And avoid anything that could be construed as argumentative: "You like the Yankees? I think they're poorly managed and don't have a chance at the World Series." You may be right, but unless you're interviewing for a job in major-league baseball, confine those arguments to your baseball-loving buddies.

Displaying loyalty is good business etiquette. Never bad-mouth former employers and colleagues, refrain from discussing other offers you've had, and don't give away trade secrets.

Leaving a job demands good business etiquette, too. Exit gracefully; don't compromise your chances for a good reference. Be cooperative, and do everything you can to help your replacement.

Proper etiquette, business and personal, is mostly a matter of common sense. That does not mean, however, that it should be approached only intuitively. Like many things in life, there are rules to be followed, and these rules shift as our world changes. There are many sources of information about proper etiquette in the workplace, and I recommend that, in addition to learning the skills necessary for your chosen career, you take the time and make the effort to gain a firm grasp of proper etiquette in today's crazy world.

Reminders on Business Etiquette

≡ Good etiquette means caring about other people.

≡ Job seekers who don't know proper etiquette come off as unsure in all ways.

≡ Once you learn what proper everyday etiquette is, you never have to worry about it again.

≡ Order simple foods during an interview lunch.

≡ Don't drink and don't smoke!

≡ Don't bring anyone with you to the interview.

≡ Be on time. In fact, be early, and use the extra time to prepare yourself.

≡ Shake hands firmly, but don't overdo it. Maintain eye contact, but don't overdo that either.

≡ Send a thank-you note right after the interview. Include something positive about you that you "forgot" to bring up during the interview.

≡ Be pleasant and courteous to everyone. A secretary or receptionist can torpedo your chances. Learn the rules about business etiquette between the "two major sexes."

≡ Etiquette is, in essence, courtesy as practiced between two human beings. The "rules" of etiquette make life easier for everyone. Playing by the rules means that everyone involved in any type of human interaction knows what behavior is appropriate.

4 · NO DREAM JOBS

A dream job is often a rude awakening

AN IRONIC PHENOMENON HAS DEVELOPED IN THE attitude of many job seekers these days. As mergers, takeovers, leveraged buyouts, lean staffs, and foreign competition become more of a harsh reality, job seekers are demanding more from the jobs they go after. They seek a "dream job." The problem is that no such job exists.

Perhaps they're dreaming as a way to mitigate the harsh reality. Perhaps they were brought up to believe in such things as dream jobs, as part of dream lives.

Psychotherapists' offices are filled these days with men and women in their thirties who, after being shielded from reality all their lives, suddenly have to face it and are ill equipped for the task.

For someone seeking a better job, the notion that a dream job awaits gets in the way of finding job fulfillment and, by extension, creates careers that are characterized by floundering, constant job changes, and, in the end, overall disappointment. Invariably these people end up blaming "the system" for their lack of success, and avoid turning inward in search of real causes for their disappointing careers.

The Me Generation's need for instant gratification

hinders many who would otherwise build solid and successful long-term careers. Big success (loosely defined, perhaps, as ending up in a dream job) results from a series of smaller successes over time. We all read of those few who start at the top, and we're envious as we toil in the lower levels of our chosen professions and occupations. The problem with starting at the top is that it doesn't prepare you for staying there. It isn't a matter of having to pay those proverbial dues before achieving great success. That sounds too much like a mandatory rite of suffering, although there is substantial benefit to be derived from dues-paying. Rather, starting at a more traditional lower level in a profession or occupation and working our way up through the various levels and layers of responsibility gives us a solid and comprehensive understanding of those levels and layers.

The irony of today's workplace is manifest everywhere we look. Jobs go begging, even though there are people out of work. Fast-food operations are offering unprecedented hourly wages and still are understaffed, sometimes having to resort to busing in workers from other areas. The trucking industry has thousands of trucks sitting idle because there aren't enough drivers. Our health care delivery system is strained, in part because of an acute shortage of nurses, many of whom have forsaken the profession. The same situation holds true for teachers. In the case of nurses and teachers, the lack of fair pay and public appreciation for the important contributions they make has driven gifted professionals out of those careers and discouraged many young people from entering them.

It's important that we evaluate jobs and professions realistically. In the case of teachers and nurses, their perceptions are supported by too many unfortunate facts. Yet others—probably including some nurses and teachers— might view their job opportunities from a less than realistic perspective, perhaps seeing them through the dark, almost opaque glasses that those in search of a dream job prefer to wear throughout their careers. Whatever happened to rose-colored glasses, through which most things look pretty good? The glass is half empty for too many people in today's job market. It used to be half full for the majority of people who held decent jobs, were paid decent salaries, and were offered realistic and fair chances for advancement.

People who enter the job market expecting to find that elusive dream job are not only doomed to a lifetime of disappointment, they are practicing planned avoidance of the realities of this world, crazy or not. They're copping out, denying reality, and not experiencing the rewards of acknowledging reality and dealing with the problems it creates. For them, reality is just an excuse for failure and inadequate performance.

A job mirrors life. If we go through life expecting an absence of problems, we end up unhappy, because that's what life is—a series of problems to be solved. If we go through our careers expecting jobs that are problem-free, that demand little effort and pay a lot, we miss the point, and we fail.

The man or woman seeking a better job must first accept the world for what it is. I can hear people saying after reading this book, "That's why I'm a failure. This world is crazy." That won't be true, but they'll take comfort in wrapping themselves in the warm blanket of placing blame. The fact is, many of the situations that contribute to this crazy world also provide new opportunities for success. Consider new industries that have blossomed in order to solve today's problems:

≡ Waste disposal. We are drowning in our own garbage. Today's bright and educated men and women will address this problem and, it is hoped, solve it, and a vast new recycling industry will prosper and preserve our environment.

≡ Crime. The need for security on all levels of life increases daily. Computer crime poses a huge threat not only to businesses but to national defense.

≡ Education. As we fall further behind the educational systems of competing nations, an assault on this problem, on every level, is inevitable. New ways of teaching, utilizing computer technology, will come out of this.

≡ Taxation. Despite claims that our system of taxation is being simplified, the reverse is blatantly true. Companies can no longer plan their future because they don't know what future tax changes will be enacted. Never before have those in the areas of finance, accounting, and tax law been so needed.

≡ Travel. Air travel is chaotic, at best, since deregulation. New and innovative approaches will have to be made.

The list could go on and on. With every change in society that contributes to its problems—to its craziness —new opportunities develop. Any person seeking a better job in this job market cannot blame the world for his or her failure. Opportunities are there, just as they have always been. Seeing this world as positive rather than negative is the first step.

What is a dream job?

Truly successful, happy people understand that the idea is to balance one's life with employment that is *tolerable* and profitable and matches our capabilities. Simultaneously, our personal lives must be brought into balance to offset some of the inevitable problems caused by our employment.

Successful, happy people are those who seek, and find, the positive aspects of their present jobs, people who overlook deficiencies. These people know that no job is perfect; no boss is an ideal human being and manager. They practice loyalty to their current employers by working hard, giving it their all, while looking to the future and preparing for their next move.

Abraham Maslow, the pioneering psychologist, studied people who were happy and well adjusted, rather than focusing on those who weren't. He found that happy people enjoy "peak experiences" in their everyday lives. They take pleasure in the task at hand, no matter how far removed it might be from the dream job they hope to get one day. When our working lives are viewed in this positive light, a more realistic evaluation of how successful we *really* are emerges. For well-adjusted, realistic people, our dream job is often the one we're doing right now. We just have to open ourselves to that possibility.

I've conducted many surveys of the American workplace. Some of the results are as amusing as they are dismaying. One survey asked management to come up with the most unusual job demands job candidates had made of them. Some were funny, some outlandish, but one sticks in my mind as symbolizing the attitude of many of today's job seekers. This individual asked to be paid extra for any time spent "thinking about work" at night or on weekends.

The person who will land a better job should be eager to learn, to grow, to contribute, and to succeed. And should be *thinking*, "If I get this job, I'll be more than happy to think about it when necessary on nights and weekends."

It's important that the seeker of a better job shed any

myths about what is "better." One such myth that has increasingly been discredited is that every job change must represent a move up. More and more Americans, particularly in middle management, are finding success and satisfaction by moving laterally within their profession. I'm not suggesting that everyone aspire to nothing more than a series of lateral moves, but I would recommend that such opportunities not be dismissed. Good middle managers who have come to the point at which they're unlikely to find promotion opportunities in their present company should certainly look to offer their services in the same position to other firms. There are, of course, many other reasons to make a lateral move. If you're the marketing manager for a company whose culture and atmosphere make you unhappy, seek the same job in a competing company or in another industry, even if the move does not represent an increase in pay and title. If you aren't happy where you are, don't think that the only move you can make is an upward one. Up doesn't necessarily translate into better.

What then, *is* a dream job?

It is employment in a field we enjoy, one that allows us to use our education, skills, and knowledge. It is a job that gives us a reasonable level of security, a decent environment in which to work, a chance to grow as professionals and as human beings, a job that will give us a reasonable sense of self-esteem and self-fulfillment, and that pays a fair wage—enough to enable us to enjoy our nonworking hours, to dress nicely, drive a functional automobile, take a regular vacation, and raise our families in decent surroundings.

That is a dream job.

You may be working at it already. If you think you're not, remind yourself to be realistic.

Reminders About Dream Jobs

≣ Big success results from a series of smaller successes over time.

≣ A job, like life, is a series of problems to be solved.

≣ People usually fail because of themselves, not because of the system in which they function.

≣ Don't discount lateral moves in your quest for a better job.

≣ You may be working in your dream job right now and not even know it. Wake up!

5 · ANALYZE YOURSELF

What do you want to be when you grow up?

THAT QUESTION IS ANSWERED DIFFERENTLY these days from when I was a young man looking to the future. I suppose the difference comes, in part, from the same lack of reality that sends many of today's young people in search of a dream job.

I met a young woman who'd just graduated from a fine university. She'd majored in journalism, as many people her age had after the glamorous Watergate years of Woodward and Bernstein. Journalism was "in." I asked her what she intended to do with her education. She answered pleasantly: "I know I don't want to work for trade magazines or in PR." She hadn't worked at anything yet. "Actually, I'd like to get into broadcasting."

"Was that part of your curriculum in school?"

"No."

"Did you work at the college radio and television stations?"

"No, but I think I'd be happier in broadcasting than writing for a newspaper. There's less writing in radio and TV. I hate to write."

People who find working with numbers boring shouldn't become accountants. If they *are* accountants, they should use their background as a trail to something else—such as selling tax services to the accounting profession.

Sound overly simple?

It should be, but isn't to a lot of employees seeking better jobs. Countless people choose professions and occupations because they're "glamorous," or because they offer big money, or because their parents want them to, without paying any regard to whether or not they are equipped to enter that field.

Members of a graduating MBA class from a prestigious Ivy League university were surveyed as to their future occupational plans. Seventy percent answered "investment banking." Whether they were qualified—investment banking, in their minds, really doesn't demand many specific skills—is less important than their reasons for making this choice. I'm certain that most of them chose the field because of the recent press about how young people are making big money in it. It's my contention that to be successful and fulfilled over the span of one's working life, there has to be a better motivation than just making big money for contributing little.

What are you really interested in? That's the first question you have to answer as you seek a better job. I became an accountant and enjoyed working in the field. I also had a desire to start a business. I had an intense interest in people and was fascinated by the process of filling jobs. I combined the two and, much to the dismay of my family and in-laws, my wife, Maxine, and I started the first personnel service specializing in filling financial and data processing positions. In fact, it was the first specialized personnel service of any type.

Because I've always loved what I do, it never occurred to me to bemoan late hours and weekend work. The standard response to this is that because it was my own business, I had a greater stake in its outcome than if I had been employed by someone. There is some obvious truth to that, but not nearly as much as we like to think. An employee who will be successful works for an employer as though that business were indeed his or her own. The key, of course, is to enjoy what you're doing—and that demands entering a profession or occupation that matches up with your needs and interests.

There are millions of people who want to be writers, yet never write anything.

College graduates want to eventually become CEOs of major companies, yet don't take the time and effort to prepare themselves with the qualifications necessary to achieve that level of success. People seeking better jobs often wait for one to come to them, rather than going after the jobs. They wait for "luck." It never seems to arrive, so they consider themselves unlucky.

"I could have been, except for..." Fill in the blank with your own excuses.

People with shaky hands should not enter dental school.

People who suffer motion sickness should not pursue the goal of being the first man or woman to land on Mars.

It isn't always easy for us to evaluate ourselves objectively. What we see when we look in the mirror doesn't necessarily reflect how other people see us. Because of this, it often makes sense to seek others' opinion of our skills and interests, hopefully more objective than our own self-evaluation, or the kind evaluation of us by friends and family. Avail yourself of guidance and career counseling services in your area. Many offer testing services to give you a more focused and unbiased analysis of your true career potential in any given profession or job area. There are a number of books that accurately describe jobs and fields of work; a careful reading will give you a pretty good indication of what's demanded of individuals seeking success in those fields.

Be open-minded when using such services. You may be told that the last profession you should consider is medicine, yet you've wanted to be a doctor since you were five years old. That doesn't mean you have to shelve that aspiration, but at least you'll be aware that it probably is going to be more difficult for you than for others whose natural interests and abilities lend themselves to the medical profession.

Probably the most important consideration is whether a profession or occupation "turns you on." Of course, you'll have to be reasonable when pursuing a career in such an area of employment when its demands are viewed against who and what you are, your strengths, weaknesses, interests, likes and dislikes.

Analyze your *real* motivations and the *real* you.

Then get moving.

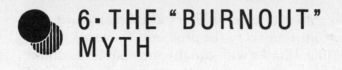

6 · THE "BURNOUT" MYTH

Burnout? Cop-out!

ONE MANIFESTATION OF THE ME GENERATION that I'm happy to see go is the concept of "burnout," a modern label for workers who experience vague depression about their jobs, a lack of energy, and waning enthusiasm for their work. The term *burnout* has become fashionable, and is worn by some people almost as a badge of honor. By claiming they burned out, they are basically saying that they are so indispensable, so good at their jobs, so dedicated, that they succumbed to the inherent stress.

Frankly, I often view this concept as a possible excuse for lowered performance. That's why I sometimes substitute the term *cop-out* for *burnout*.

What happened, it seems to me, is that as our work ethics slipped, and more men and women sought greater pay for less hours, the idea of working extra hours became anathema to them. It didn't take much for some of them to "burn out." In prior generations, many workers put in exceedingly long hours, postponed vacations too often, and, as a result, suffered from the natural fatigue that accompanies that sort of schedule. The remedy was to take a vacation, and to learn to enjoy slack periods a

41

little more. Many of these workers also became aware of their own contribution to the problem. They took on impossibly difficult tasks with equally impossible deadlines, and, as a result, the quality of the work perhaps slipped. But those overworked men and women did not talk about being burned out. Instead, they said, "I'm tired...I need a day off."

Webster defines *burn out* in its literal sense: "To burn till the fuel is exhausted and the fire ceases." That makes sense to me when applied to flames in a fireplace, but not when applied to worker productivity.

Do people really burn out? I don't think so. I assume that the burnout trend began with such professions as teachers, law enforcement officers, and nurses—professions in which good performance often is rewarded by frustration and disillusionment. Cops arrest a criminal and see him or her walk free because of an overly lenient judicial system. Teachers watch their pupils refuse to learn or to behave responsibly. Nurses minister to patients and too often see their dedication and skill rewarded not by deserved increases in pay, but by a lack of respect from a variety of people, including the doctors with whom they work. And, of course, added to the nurses' plight is having to deal with inevitably seeing many of their patients die.

While the frustration of people in these professions is certainly understandable, I still take issue with applying a term such as *burnout* to them. In some cases I think this label was used by certain factions within their forces to create a justification for longer vacations for teachers, shorter shifts for nurses, and higher pay for policemen.

What's being debated here is not whether the stress of our busy working lives, coupled with the tensions of this fast-paced society in which we must function, doesn't take its toll. Stress in the workplace is simply an extension of stress caused by living. Adults must learn to cope with stress in their daily lives, and the same coping mechanisms must be applied in the workplace. That reality, however, isn't good enough reason in this day and age to throw up our hands, claim to be burned out, and expect others to accept this excuse for poor performance and lack of initiative. That might have been the case when times were fat in American industry. Now every employee must not only do his or her job, but expend extra effort and drive to help American companies compete globally. This leaves little room for anyone with a tendency to burn out when the pressure is on.

If you are someone who burned out in past jobs, take whatever steps are necessary to correct the situation. The first is to realize that those who claim to be burned out are really claiming that they are victims. Quite the opposite is true. People who function at a high level of productivity, who thrive on deadlines and view the stress of any occupation as a challenge, never consider themselves victims of anything. *They* are in control. They make efficient use of their time, and set realistic deadlines instead of letting external factors dictate to them. They're honest with themselves, and are quick to admit certain factors in them that contribute to lowered performance and job dissatisfaction. An accountant who sees only numbers will quickly claim to be burned out through repetition and lack of challenge. Another accountant viewing those same numbers sees them as representing a story, something larger than numbers on a sheet of paper.

Challenge the concept of burnout. Today's better jobs don't leave any room for it.

Reminders About "Burning Out"

≡ Burnout? Cop-out!

≡ Our "golden age" didn't work. The work ethic is back. Too often, claiming to be burned out is nothing more than an excuse for lowered performance.

≡ People who burn out are of little use to today's lean-and-mean, competitive companies.

≡ If you think you are prone to burning out, take steps to correct it before it gets in the way of finding a better job.

≡ Learn to take control of your own life. People who do that never think about becoming burned out.

7 · FORGET LUCK

People who work hard at being lucky are
the luckiest people

More people will give you credit for your "good luck"
than for your genius, knowledge, skills,
and hard work.

AN ACQUAINTANCE OF MINE GAVE BIRTH TO A
daughter on my birthday. I visited her in the hospital,
and she said to me, "I hope my daughter is as lucky as
you have been."

I felt a twinge of resentment (only a twinge; she certainly didn't mean to be disparaging). I told the story to
another friend, a man who had become successful
through years of dedication and hard work. He laughed,
and told me that he'd suffered a lot more than just a
twinge of resentment when one of his sons spent an evening espousing the theory that just about all success results from a stroke of luck, being in the right place at the
right time.

People seeking a better job in today's world will be as
lucky in succeeding as they are determined to find success. The pessimists will always consider any lack of success an indication of how unlucky they are. The optimists

will keep wishing for good luck, but will do little to create it. And the self-motivated man or woman will always seem to be lucky to the rest.

The term *luck* has its place. There's luck involved in winning a game of bingo. Buying one card with which to play is fine, except that by buying two cards you increase your odds of winning. Four cards give you better odds of winning than two cards, and so on. I don't believe in luck when it comes to finding a better job. Improving your *odds* is another matter. People who send a résumé to two firms seeking their particular skills and knowledge have a 100 percent better chance than a similarly skilled and knowledgeable person who applies only to one firm.

Successful men and women create their own luck.

Here's one person's story that brings home the point and is worthy of analyzing:

A friend of a friend of mine, a woman, had entered the work force about ten years ago, after having brought up her children and having been divorced. Her education had been strong in writing and journalism, so she sought out and got a job with a local newspaper. It didn't pay much, but she attacked it as though she were working for the *Wall Street Journal,* and being paid big money. At the same time, she networked with everyone with whom she came into contact and began doing free-lance writing on the side. This broadened her circle of professional contacts, each of whom saw that she was a hard worker, was skilled at her craft, was open to new opportunities, and was determined to make full use of her potential.

A successful local company was looking for a director of public relations. One of her circle of contacts knew of the opening, called her, and asked if she would be interested in applying for the job. She applied and was hired. At the same time, she expanded her free-lance activities (always on her own time, of course), and her professional circle of advocates continued to grow, which meant even more people who were impressed with her abilities and approach.

Five years later, one of these professional associates called and informed her that a major company was seeking a director of public relations, with the promise of becoming a vice-president within a year. Here's where I came in.

Because this woman had read some of the books and columns I've written on career success (her access to them basically came through my friend, with whom I'd had a working relationship for a number of years), she dug into them again in search of the right steps to take in pursuing this plum of a job, for which there were many qualified candidates.

She'd put into motion a few years ago the first step she was to take, which was to look into the file she'd kept on herself over the past five years. I've always advocated the keeping of a "personal personnel file," in which your achievements on the job, major contributions to the company, ideas that worked, and other things like that are noted and saved. By doing this, she was able to quickly identify items that should be included on her updated résumé.

She took care to follow the basic rules for preparing an effective résumé (covered later in this book), and made sure it was error-free by having more than one set of eyes proofread it.

Instead of simply mailing her résumé and cover letter, she sent them by Federal Express, even though the company to which she was applying was only thirty miles away. She wouldn't have gone to this trouble and expense if she had been applying to many firms, but this was a job she wanted and knew she was highly qualified for. By using an air courier, she ensured that the people on the receiving end would *know* she was applying, and headed off any chance of "It must have been lost in the mailroom" excuses being given for not receiving it. She'd already caused herself to stand out from the other candidates.

She followed up a few days later with a phone call, in which she confirmed that she was indeed extremely interested in the position.

She prepared for her initial interview with great care, using a chapter from one of my books as a guide. She rehearsed her answers to probable questions, knew exactly the selling points about herself she wished to get across no matter what questions were asked, and spent time in the library learning everything she could about the company and its top people.

She arrived very early for the interview, and used the time to sip a leisurely cup of coffee in a nearby coffee shop, rather than running the risk of being late because of heavy traffic or trouble in finding the company's location.

She followed all the other rules I've laid out over the years about how to conduct oneself during an interview (the subject of a later chapter).

The interview went well. She returned home and wrote a brief note to the man who'd interviewed her, thanking him for his time and courtesy, and indicating that she was now even more enthusiastic about the job.

She let a few days go by before sending him a second note. This time, rather than simply writing another thank-you letter, she used the note to bring up something about herself that had not been discussed in the interview but that she thought might be of interest to him.

She was called in for a second interview. Things were looking good, but there were still a number of finalists.

Again she allowed a few days to pass, during which she looked for something in a newspaper or a trade journal that her potential boss might not have seen but would find of interest. She found it and mailed it off. She had been asked during the second interview to provide five references. Instead of coming up with them on the spot, she'd said she would send them in the next day, after she had a chance to call each one, out of courtesy. She prepared the list, called those on it, and had it messengered in the following morning, again not trusting it to the erratic postal system. Of course, she knew that the five people she'd selected would say positive things about her—not because they were friends, but because they didn't have a reason to say anything negative. She also knew that, should the company seek its own reference list, she had nothing to fear. Her résumé was scrupulously honest—no overstating of responsibilities, no gaps to cover up, no skeletons in her closet. She'd presented herself, both on paper and in person, with total honesty, always putting her best foot forward, of course, but without unnecessary embellishment.

She was called again and asked when she could start if she was hired. It was down to two people now, this woman and one other person. She said she would like to give her present employer a month's notice, out of fairness and the need to help train a new person. That might be a problem, she was told. There was a major project to be written. They'd need to get started on it in less than a month. Her answer: if she was hired, she would use weekends and nights to work on the project while still with her present employer.

That did it. She was hired.

Now, think of all the "luck" this woman was the recipient of. I can hear the comments from those job seekers who trust to luck.

"She knew somebody. She had an 'in.'"

Of course she knew somebody. She'd worked hard at

knowing people in her professional sphere, people who knew of opportunities and might pass them along to her. It wasn't a calculated meeting of people who could do something for her, however. Many of these professional associates had become friends. By keeping in contact with them, she enhanced her knowledge of the field and kept up with changes in it. Yes, she knew someone, but it wasn't luck that she did. Far from it.

I was delighted that she used some of my advice as a basis for pursuing this job, but knowing me isn't the point. What is important is that she sought out and used every available resource, in this case my books and columns. My books and columns are available to *anyone*, along with the books and columns of many other men and women knowledgeable in the areas of employment and career success. This woman took the time and effort to learn everything she could that would enhance her chances of being hired for that coveted job.

No, I don't put any stock in luck when it comes to landing a better job. I much prefer to speak of odds than luck.

The woman in my example did everything possible to cut down the odds against her and move the advantage to her side. This is crucial for anyone seeking a better job these days.

As I said before, companies are more reluctant than ever to hire smokers, because some bosses will not allow smokers in their department. People who don't smoke naturally improve their odds in today's job market—perhaps only slightly, but enough to be worthwhile. Heavy drinking, too, is definitely out. Those who insist upon following the old style cut their odds of being successful.

Learn from losers. It has always been my contention that while studying and emulating successful people has great value for men and women looking to succeed, there is actually more to be learned from those who failed. We all know people who just never seem to get anywhere, never find the sort of success they want. Often we say these people have bad luck, but we also know that luck can't be the only reason. Take a close look at them; analyze the way they go about things, the approach they take, the attitudes they exhibit. The flaws and weaknesses are usually apparent. By vowing to keep those negatives out of our lives, we've taken a positive step in improving our odds.

Success doesn't stem from luck. The dictionary definition of luck is: "the seemingly chance happening of events which affect one."

Success isn't a chance happening. It's the result of hard work, long-term career planning, and the decision to strike *luck* from the job seeker's vocabulary.

Reminders About "Luck"

≡ If luck seems to have played a role in people finding a better job, it's because they worked hard to create their "good luck."

≡ Work hard at whatever job you currently have. "Lucky" people always work hard.

≡ Network, network, network.

≡ Learn how to look for a better job.

≡ Keep your own personal personnel file.

≡ Prepare your résumé with care.

≡ Send your résumé by messenger or air courier if it's a job you really want and you match its specs.

≡ Follow up. Send a thank-you note. Stay in touch.

≡ Follow the rules for a successful interview. (See chapter 21.)

≡ Be honest on your résumé and in what you say during the interview.

≡ Choose your references carefully, and obtain their permission.

≡ Be willing to begin your new job part time, and without pay, if necessary. Do everything you can to improve your odds, but eliminate *luck* from your vocabulary.

8 · THE JOB MARKET

The job market dropped dead!

IF I'VE HEARD THE FOLLOWING ONCE IN MY forty-plus years in the personnel services business, I've heard it a thousand times.

A job candidate comes in to one of our 150 offices. He's brimming with confidence. He tells one of our placement counselors that he's already been on four very successful interviews, but wants to see as many potential employers as possible before deciding which job he'll take. "The job market is great out there," he says. We suggest a few possibilities, but he decides not to bother pursuing them. They're beneath his standards. (In most cases, he's conjured up standards far above what the reality of his credentials dictates.)

A month or two later, he shows up and tells our counselor, "The job market has dropped dead out there."

What happens in this situation is very much like what happens when we sell a house. We put it up for sale, and in the first few weeks there are serious potential buyers. Some make offers, which we turn down because, based upon what we've seen during those initial weeks, "There's a terrific market out there for our house."

Then the stream dwindles into a trickle; we're

53

lucky if we see one somewhat interested buyer every month.
What is a "market"?

When we put a house up for sale, we immediately
attract that group of people who are actively looking for a
house at that moment. Some have just started their
search for a new house. Some have been looking for a
house similar to ours for a week, a month, a year, or even
longer. They are the so-called market for that house. Once
they have passed through and have decided to keep looking, the "terrific market" vanishes.

The same holds true when you're looking for a job.
The market for you consists of the openings available
when you start to look. As with the sale of a house, some
companies just started to look for someone like you;
others have been looking for a week, a month, a year, or
longer. More than that, the job market is defined by those
companies whose needs generally fit what you, the job
seeker, have to offer. It's a tiny market at best, and once
you've gone through it—and failed to connect with a job
—it disappears.

Don't be too independent, especially if you're unemployed or about to be unemployed. It could take many
months to come up with a solid offer.

There are, of course, clearly defined job markets.
Often they're geographic. Mass layoffs at the largest plant
in a small town, or its closing, create a truly depressed
job market. Conversely, the opening of a major new plant
creates a generally positive job market for a wide array of
workers in the area. Cutbacks in certain programs by federal and state governments can produce a depressed job
market in specified fields, just as increases in government
budgets can create the reverse effect.

I remember once driving with my wife from San
Diego to Los Angeles. We were listening to the radio and
heard that a major retailer in California was closing all of

its operations, which meant laying off eight thousand people within the year. The newscaster interviewed four of the employees who were about to lose their jobs and asked them what plans they'd made to find another position. None of them had made any plans. In effect, they were all waiting, burying their heads in the sand, hoping something good would come up between then and the time they received their last paycheck. That meant that at some point virtually all eight thousand laid-off employees would be looking for a new job at the same time.

Anyone working for a company that has announced its intention to close, even though it doesn't plan to do so for a year, should begin looking immediately and should, from the day of the announcement, consider himself or herself unemployed.

Sometimes companies will be so generous with severance pay that they create a false sense of security. Not too long ago, a major corporation laid off a number of people in Florida, giving them what amounted to a year's salary and various other considerations that created in these employees a lack of urgency about finding other work. As in the case of the California retailer, these employees didn't start looking immediately, because they would lose that year's pay. So what? Better to have a new position than to plan to live off a severance package. The fact is, a year goes by quickly. Not only that, it is much easier to find a better job while you are employed than if you begin to look after you're out of work.

For most people seeking a better job, the job market means what that individual has to offer to a small group of companies that might need such skills and experience.

Many people use the concept of a job market as an excuse for their lack of success, or for their unwillingness to energetically pursue a career in their chosen field. The young woman I mentioned earlier—the one who wanted broadcast journalism—also said, "I can't find a job in journalism. Everybody got into it."

Nonsense! We heard the same story about young people who wanted to become teachers in the seventies. They were told that the teaching profession was glutted and they'd never find a job. By the time those who didn't listen to such advice graduated with degrees in teaching and entered the work force, the field had opened up and there was a great demand for good teachers—a demand that is even more acute today.

"Any luck?" a friend asks someone who has been job hunting.

"No, the market stinks."

For the steelworker in a depressed area, that might be a valid claim. For most of us trying to find better jobs, it doesn't hold water.

The job market! It is as depressed and narrow as people think it is.

The number of men and women who are narrowing their own job market these days is appalling. That young journalism graduate drastically narrowed her job potential by immediately ruling out working for trade magazines or in PR, even though they are two splendid entry-level possibilities in which the writing craft can be sharpened, the experience of working as a writer can be gained, and the beginnings of a network of fellow professionals can be launched.

Rigidity works against you, especially early in a business career. Successful people are constantly finding themselves deviating from their early career plans. *Working Woman* magazine did a survey of six thousand working women. Only 8 percent of those women were doing what they had originally planned to do in their careers. Don't rule out any options. If you do, you stand a good chance of missing that proverbial golden opportunity.

I've heard it over and over again. There are job seekers who decide that they will work only in a certain section of the city, because the restaurants are better there. They will not travel more than fifteen minutes from home. They must have a private office with a window, southern exposure preferred; medical benefits must include dental and psychotherapy; if the company won't pay for their MBA until after they've been there a year, forget it; they demand generous vacation plans, a day off for their mother-in-law's birthday, a specified make and model of company car—no substitutions; and on and on. I haven't made these up. We've done surveys of employers to pinpoint the most outlandish requests made by job seekers, and these only scratch the surface.

A crazy world?

Crazy people?

The man or woman who will find a better job will bring to an employer a keen sense of loyalty, ethics, and a desire to be productive, to contribute to that company's success. Young people entering the work force will abandon the old army adage "Volunteer for nothing" and will volunteer for almost everything. They'll adopt the philosophy "First In, Last Out" (FILO). Like the pendulum of ethics and loyalty, the pendulum of worker productivity is beginning its arc back toward a more productive and efficient workplace. Those who have been content to "beat the system" by doing as little as possible for as much money as possible will find themselves left behind. It's inevitable. America, and its economic life, can't settle for anything less.

As industry tires (and wilts) under a couple of generations of Me Generation workers, the older segment of our population is returning in droves to the factory, the fast-food outlet, and the office. The decreasing population of young people contributes to this growing trend. The U.S.

Census Bureau estimates that by 2000 our eighteen-to-twenty-four age group will shrink by 4 million people, while our over-forty-five segment will increase by 23 million. In surveys, more than half of retired workers over the age of seventy have indicated that they want to return to work. Obviously, our older population is becoming a necessary and valued labor pool for American industry.

But employers are finding added benefits in hiring older people. These men and women came up when the work ethic was firmly established, and they tend to live by it. They're loyal, and they carry the ethical strength of their generation into today's work environment. They'll be taking an increasing number of jobs, which means younger people seeking better jobs will have them to compete with, as well as their peers.

If you're an older person looking for a better job, keep squarely in mind how much you're needed these days. There often is a tendency for older people to approach the process of job hunting with a less confident, almost apologetic posture. This is not only true of men and women who have retired and are seeking to return to work, it's a common problem with executives on the "wrong" side of forty who assume they're over the hill, unable to compete with younger executives.

Older men and women seeking better jobs are sometimes actually embarrassed to be looking for work, and being interviewed by younger people. If *you* suffer that feeling, remind yourself that you bring experience, perception, and stability to a company—vitally important traits for younger managers looking to enhance their own careers through the work of those they supervise. You must, of course, curb any temptation to lord over a younger prospective boss the fact that you have many years' experience and, by extension, might know more about the job than he or she does. If anyone needs to exhibit the team-player attitude, it's the older worker. The new and younger management of a company will be doing things their way, which may well be different from the way you did it. Adopt the philosophy that the new way might be better and that you'll find the means to meld your long experience into the new structure.

Another thing I've noticed about older workers is a reluctance to network. Older men and women often view networking as asking for favors. No matter what your age, if you're seeking a better job, you should go after it using all the ideas and techniques I've suggested in this book, just as younger men and women will be doing.

Make sure you aren't in a rut, particularly if you're out of work. Often this is exactly the time to consider a change in your career. Most people who make a career change in midstream do it after they've been a success for a number of years. They have the benefit of experience, are better able to evaluate their needs and goals, and, presumably, have stashed away enough money to support a transition. Being fired could be viewed as an opportunity to take stock and to set out on the career path that will make you happiest and most productive during the latter portion of your working life.

For younger people seeking better jobs, having a growing legion of older workers with whom to compete is another example of this crazy world. Who would have believed it would happen? At the same time, it makes the point that the term *crazy* doesn't always mean something negative. In the case of *this* "craziness," it's welcome.

Reminders About the Job Market

≡ Be realistic when evaluating the job market for what you have to offer.

≡ The job market always looks great at first; it dries up fast.

≡ The minute you know you will be laid off at a future date, consider yourself unemployed.

≡ Don't blame a so-called bad job market for your failure to find a job. Look for ways to create a new job market for yourself.

≡ Don't be too narrow in how you view a job market. Be flexible, open to new ideas and possibilities.

≡ If you're an older person, view the positive aspects of your experience and stability, rather than considering yourself over the hill.

≡ If you end up with a younger boss, be flexible enough to incorporate your skills and experience into the way they do things.

≡ If you need to look for a job later in life, view it as an opportunity to analyze whether it's time to shift gears and get out of any rut you might have slipped into.

9·FINDING BETTER JOBS WHERE YOU ARE

The grass may be browner somewhere else

AS WE ALL KNOW, THERE ARE ASPECTS OF LIVING on this earth over which we have little or no control. The severe drought of the summer of 1988 is an example.

So is the global economic situation, which has dramatically changed the way we do business. As more of America is owned by foreign firms and investors, and other nations become increasingly efficient and supportive of their industries, our business and industry leaders must shift gears even to stay close to being competitive. Those of you who will find better jobs in the midst of this chaos will have to understand that, as one of Duke Ellington's famous songs says, "Things Ain't What They Used to Be."

The Japanese system of management has had a profound impact on American industry. It is being adopted (after being modified somewhat to suit deep-seated American values) by companies across the United States. The continuation, as well as the growing acceptance of this, is as inevitable as the 1988 drought, or any other natural phenomenon over which we have little or no control. We can, however, use the Japanese "invasion" to our advantage. We can accept and understand the reality it repre-

61

sents, and include our understanding of it in what we offer prospective employers.

In 1983, things were going poorly for Delta Airlines. The executives and board members took a pay cut. So did rank-and-file employees. Not only that, the employees donated money to the company to buy a new $30 million jet aircraft. Whether members of management at Delta had studied the Japanese system of management or not, the result was an approach that represented a classic Japanese management answer to a problem. Delta's top management actually received a call from leading Japanese business leaders to ascertain where in Japan they'd studied their management techniques. Today, Delta is considered one of our most successful and best-managed airlines.

Because of the 1988 drought, farmers must find new ways to irrigate, and drought insurance (sometimes called rain insurance) will be part of more farmers' planning in the years ahead.

For the job seeker, the change in the way we do business in America means that we must change our thinking, as well as some of our approaches to finding better employment. The first thing anyone seeking a better job must do is understand how things have changed and, to the best of his or her ability, predict where things will go in the future.

One aspect of the Japanese management style is the concept of lifetime employment. That concept used to apply to millions of Americans a few decades ago, but has been killed off of late, in part by our takeover and merger mania. Headlines say it all: a communications company cuts twenty-seven thousand from its payroll; a computer company lets ten thousand go; a car manufacturer chops twenty-nine thousand. Hardly conducive to fostering employee commitment to staying a lifetime at any one company. We've become a paranoid work force, and for good reason. We've become a nation of job hoppers largely because of the unstable business climate that has been created.

Yet there are still many companies in which loyal employees *do* stay a lifetime and are rewarded for it. I predict we'll see more of this as the Japanese management style takes further hold on the way we manage our own businesses and, of course, as more Japanese industries are set up here in the United States.

Consequently, I suggest that, before *assuming* that the only way to find a better job is to look outside your present employment, you first realistically evaluate the potential available to you where you're presently employed. The grass isn't always greener somewhere else. In fact, considering the instability of many companies, the grass may not even be growing someplace else.

Before deciding to look for a better job outside your present company, take a look inside. View your current employer the same way you would view a prospective new employer. In other words, spend some time *seeking* a new and better job without jumping into the unknown. Apply the same principles of looking for a new job right where you are: establishing high visibility, networking, sharpening skills that will make you more useful, and selling yourself and your experience, skills, and accomplishments.

≣ Make yourself visible within your company, so that other managers in search of new staff members might consider *you*, rather than looking outside for a new person.

≣ Establish and maintain contacts with people in other divisions. See if there aren't other areas to which you could contribute, without taking away from your present responsibilities.

≡ Is there an internal employee publication? If so, seek out the chance to write for it.

≡ Sharpen your writing skills and submit material to trade magazines in your industry or profession.

≡ Become active in community organizations, as well as professional ones.

≡ Start dressing better, as though every day on the job represented a job interview. I always advise dressing slightly better than your colleagues.

≡ Make it known that you are interested in finding greater responsibilities and advancement within the company. Discuss this with your superiors—not in a complaining way, but indicating your sincere desire for success where you are.

When the grass looks greener in a neighbor's yard, it might be because you haven't taken good enough care of your own. Instead of hopping the fence, apply some extra water and fertilizer and see what happens. Your grass might end up a lot greener than next door. The same thing can be true when deciding where a better job can be found.

Reminders About Looking for Greener Grass

≡ It's still possible, and maybe preferable, to stay with one company until retirement.

≡ Look for a better job where you are now. Don't assume that all the better jobs are somewhere else.

≡ View every day on your present job as though you are being interviewed for a new one.

≡ Become visible within your company.

≡ Broaden your contacts throughout the company.

≡ Become active in community and professional organizations.

≡ Always dress slightly better than your colleagues.

≡ Learn more about your company and industry.

≡ Learn job skills that are related to yours within your company.

10 · LEARN TO BE LITERATE

A yen for success

ANYONE GIVING ADVICE TO JOB SEEKERS ADVO-cates doing your homework before applying for a job. That means researching companies to which you send résumés so that you can fine-tune your cover letter. Then, if you're lucky enough to be called in for an interview, you should do even more research on the company and its industry so that you can intelligently discuss those things and formulate sensible questions and comments. You should also, despite the difficulty involved, try to find out something about the individuals who will be interviewing you.

However, because you're looking for a better job, there's some additional homework to be done, and this involves understanding a little more about how the world works today.

It is rather ironic that the Japanese now use American workers as "cheap labor." Other ironies abound. We are said to have become a "service economy," yet our quality of service is at an all-time low. We live in an age of often mind-boggling technology, yet few of us are able to understand it to the point of using it. A good example is the incredible sophistication of weaponry in our military that requires exceptionally well educated and talented individuals to make it work. Such people are not likely to volunteer for military service in great numbers.

Our ability to communicate clearly and quickly these days is facilitated by technology that was only science-fiction speculation forty years ago. Yet so many of our young adults in the work force, including those who seem to aspire to *much* better jobs, are woefully undereducated in such things as international and domestic geography, economics, history, writing—even reading.

We've become an age of specialists, which, despite its advantages in many situations, breeds whole groups of people whose focus is only upon their specialty, without any understanding of how what they do fits into the much larger and complex puzzle of business and of life.

Consider this: it's estimated by the U.S. Department of Education that 25 million American adults—one in seven—are functional illiterates, who can't read, write, calculate, or solve problems even at a level that would allow them to accomplish simple tasks. A further estimate by the DOE indicates that there are 45 million adults working today who are either functionally or marginally illiterate. Functionally illiterate adults account for about 30 percent of unskilled workers, 29 percent of semiskilled workers, and 11 percent of all managers, professionals, and technicians. That's scary. Estimates vary, but a median figure would be that adult illiteracy costs this country an estimated $225 billion annually in lost productivity, lost tax revenues, welfare costs, prison costs, crime, and other related social ills.

What this means to you, the literate man or woman seeking a better job in this illiterate climate, is that you have a strong edge. It is hoped that you're well read and able to understand the complexities of this world—but you should also be thinking about ways to cope with this horrendous problem. Enlightened corporations are well aware of the dilemma caused by the illiteracy of some of their workers, and would welcome suggestions about how to improve the ability of their workers to understand instructions, directives, and other written information. At least, when ending up in a managerial job, take into consideration the fact that the reason one of your directives might not have been carried out is that the person reading it is marginally or even functionally illiterate, despite outward appearances.

The level of writing skills even at high management levels has deteriorated over the years I've been in the business world. Executives now dictate everything, and often depend upon a secretary to clean up their grammar and punctuation. Then many sign it, without recognizing that all dictation needs pencil editing. The tape recorder is a marvelous thing—I use it all the time to dictate notes and memos—but I would never think of having something dictated sent out without having gone over it.

If you happen to be a highly literate person, particularly in verbal and written communication, don't be smug. You might have a way with words but, at the same time, be an innumerate.

Innumerates are people who are illiterate in mathematics. The Educational Testing Service conducted an extensive survey of how math-smart our high-school students are. The results were appalling—and they were dealing with *basic* math.

We seem to be no better at teaching geography. The majority of students in another survey could not point to the United States on a world map.

Obviously, the problems of illiteracy, innumeracy, and geographical ignorance are pervasive in our work world. Imagine the edge you have by being able to communicate verbally and by the written word, and by having a basic understanding of practical mathematics and simple economics.

If I had to boil down this book to one suggestion for getting a better job in this crazy world, it would be *get smart*. And don't stop learning until you stop breathing.

Recently, a large company introduced a counseling program for employees suffering personal problems. There's nothing new about companies offering such services, except in this case the therapist the employee talks to is a computer named "Dr. Bob." It asks questions on the screen, and the employee types in the answers. Then the software program evaluates the answers and goes on to another series of questions. Dr. Bob represents "Freud on a floppy disk"; whether this will catch on in psychotherapy remains to be seen.

In the employment industry, a number of software programs have been introduced that presumably help a job seeker make career choices, write résumés, and handle other aspects of job seeking. I don't think much of these, because, like professional résumé services, they turn out a legion of cookie-cutter job candidates. By the way, some personnel offices are now using computers to initially screen job applicants. These operate on the same principle as Dr. Bob: the candidate answers questions flashed on the screen, and when the session is over the computer analyzes that person's qualifications for employment.

Whether communicating with a computer or a real live human being, the basic fact remains the same: one of the major stumbling blocks for career advancement is an inability to communicate, verbally as well as in writing. Those who will achieve success in the years ahead will be able to communicate their ideas clearly. Others, with equally good ideas, will not be listened to because they have not expressed their ideas with clarity and in a way that prompts attention from superiors. A good idea that no one knows about or can understand ends up as a no-idea.

People seeking better jobs will have to commit themselves to being more productive. Our productivity level is down, and economists agree that inflation results in part from lowered productivity. An excellent example of what has happened to us can be found in England, where for each worker employed in a Nissan plant twenty-four cars a year are turned out. Down the road, a Ford plant turns out only six cars a year for each worker employed.

The Japanese auto makers with plants in the U.S. have only four or five job classifications. At Ford, General Motors, and Chrysler, there are as many as sixty such classifications. Japanese auto plants here get as much as 50 percent more productivity from their workers than we get at comparable manufacturing facilities.

The answer is not to say that the Japanese are better than we are, nor is unionism totally to blame, although lower productivity can frequently be traced to union restrictions on productivity in certain industries. A recent study compared two work crews, each assigned the same project. One worked under its union rules; the other was nonunion. The nonunion crew worked about fifty minutes out of each hour, while the union crew worked thirty-five minutes. The union crew used eight people to get the job done, the nonunion crew five people.

Recently a Roper survey asked American, Japanese, and European workers to rank the most important aspects of their lives. For the Americans, work came in eighth place; for the Europeans, work was fourth; for the Japanese, it was second.

None of this should be construed as my pointing a

finger at labor unions and blaming them for our lack of productivity. They have contributed to it, of course. There was a time when American workers desperately needed protection from widespread long hours, low pay, and unsafe, cruel working conditions. That need doesn't seem quite as urgent any more.

What *is* important is that if the American competitive position is to be improved, employees who will find and hold better jobs will have to be more productive. The years ahead will call for and reward employees who are willing to give a little extra, to stay late and arrive early when necessary, pitch in when a colleague is absent, take some chances, and not make excuses when they fail. Successful employees are ones who commit themselves to doing things right, recognize that everyone has a boss (even the company's owner, who must answer to the customer, or top executives who must answer to shareholders) and that business is not in business to satisfy their personal needs. These people who succeed will not seek raises because a new baby is on the way. They'll make their case for raises and promotions based upon what they've contributed to the company.

At the same time, those who manage American companies will have to recognize that the world has changed (even if they prefer not to term it "crazy"), and that in order to attract and keep good people they'll have to make their own adjustments, including providing day care, ensuring that the work environment is free of sexual harassment, instituting policies that reward those who perform (as opposed to across-the-board merit raises), viewing business as a long-term endeavor rather than always seeking fatter quarterly bottom lines at the expense of customers or clients, and, in general, recognizing that the people who work for them are the key to their success or failure.

Combine the two—workers who care and who give a little extra and management that recognizes and rewards these people—and you have a less crazy world, to say nothing of one that restores our overall economy to higher profitability.

Want to get a better job?

Do whatever you must to become a skilled communicator, no matter what your focus of expertise. At least be literate. Understand that this world—the one in which you seek better jobs—creates its own demands, and that unless you understand these demands and are willing to shift your own gears in order to accommodate them, your chances of finding true success are diminished.

Read. Be able to put today's society into perspective with yesterday's times. In order to truly understand the society into which we were born, we must have some understanding of the events that went before us and that have shaped our present lives. There's an old saying: "We are what we were." Develop a broader sense of the larger world. By doing that, the way our own individual little worlds function becomes easier to understand.

A distinct error on the part of many people in today's job market is to focus in narrowly on a specific job and not take the time to keep abreast of the profession or industry as a whole. I've been an editorial adviser to the *Journal of Accountancy* for a number of years. I went through one issue and tabulated the different abbreviations and acronyms in it. There were many, and my guess is that half the professionals reading the magazine could not identify all of them.

We see it every day—bright, talented, and well-educated men and women who are virtually ignorant of what is going on in their chosen field of work. An interviewer mentions a recent bit of legislation that directly affects the direction an industry will take. It has been in all the papers, and covered in-depth in that industry's trade publications. The job applicant stares back, a blank look on his or her face. Or major appointments have been made to new positions in industry associations, but the job applicant isn't aware of this, and makes it painfully clear during the interview.

People seeking better jobs have to look beyond the "smallness" of *their* jobs and companies. Those who bother to do this have a much better chance of achieving true success than those who spend their working lives in a virtual vacuum, oblivious to the forces around them that have direct bearing upon their jobs, their companies, and their futures.

Adopt the attitude that the life you live is not a dress rehearsal. You have one life in which to achieve your personal and professional goals. Luck won't do it. Waiting for things to happen won't do it. Carrying negative attitudes into your job won't do it.

Celebrate this crazy world, and view it as filled with opportunity. Shelve the clichés, and ignore the fads. Learn how to pursue a better job. Approach job hunting and job advancement as a job in itself.

11 · BEING FIRED

It can't happen to me

ONE OUT OF EVERY FOUR OF YOU WILL BE FIRED.

I'm not referring to the loss of jobs while in college or high school. I'm talking about you—an educated, skilled, and valuable employee.

A survey we commissioned came up with the above statistic. It represents the opinions of personnel directors and top executives nationwide.

Even worse, of the 25 percent of American men and women who will be fired at some point, 20 percent will not deserve to lose their jobs.

How can this happen? Here we are, a nation locked in mortal combat with foreign competitors who are literally buying us up, defeating us in the global marketplace, and American men and women who don't deserve to lose their jobs *will* lose them. These are the same men and women who conceivably would have the answers to our competitive problems, yet they will be out of work through no fault of their own.

Has our world really gone *that* crazy?

Evidently.

Read on.

12 · BANKRUPTCIES, MERGERS, AND TAKEOVERS

Who do I work for today?

THIS CHAPTER IS ABOUT BANKRUPTCY, AS WELL AS mergers, takeovers, and leveraged buyouts, any of which can be bad for your career health. They represent reality in this day and age, and men and women who will find better jobs despite them will first understand how they happen and be ready to deal with the results.

It wasn't long ago that companies chose bankruptcy as a last resort, a legal remedy to crushing debt and, through restructuring, the chance to pull themselves out of a financial mess and continue in business. During this same era, bankruptcy carried with it a stigma; those who were forced to seek it as a shelter—businesses and individuals alike—felt a certain shame and frustration at ending up in that position.

No more. Today bankruptcy has become a management tool. Stalemates in union negotiations are broken by the company's going into Chapter 11 and forcing unions to lower demands on it when it emerges from protective bankruptcy as a "new" company. There's obviously something wrong with this from an ethical perspective, to say nothing of its damage to the economic health of the nation.

Companies tottering on the brink of bankruptcy used to be seen as losers, places for investors to stay away from. Today, in this crazy world, these companies are often seen as pots of gold for financial wheeler-dealers, who, through the popular process of leveraged buyout, can make millions (even billions) from them.

While all this probably makes sense to a new breed of financial wizard, the negative impact on the lives of millions of employees is too often ignored. I'm talking about you, the man or woman seeking a better job, or at least trying to find some security and advancement in your present job.

In 1987 there were 22,564 Chapter 11 filings under the Federal Bankruptcy Code. That's more than four times as many as in 1980. This is good news for people who know how to make money from failure. Analysts estimate that investments in the securities of companies in bankruptcy, or on the verge of bankruptcy, now exceed $20 billion, compared with $1 billion ten years ago. In other words, we now have a much greater opportunity to invest in failure, even though the *real* failure is the disservice done to all the men and women who lose their jobs in the process.

Mergers are another popular game that can lose you your job and cut down on the number of opportunities for better jobs in your future. We've become a merger-happy, takeover-crazed society. Back in 1982, the value of mergers and acquisitions reached an all-time high of $82.6 billion. By 1986 that figure was up to $190 billion. The number of takeovers valued at $1 billion or more quintupled between 1983 and 1986. Seventy-five of the hundred largest mergers in our history have occurred since 1981. Only the most blissfully naïve worker fails to understand what happens to jobs when the corporate raiders arrive. You merge two companies and you instantly have two vice-presidents of sales, two controllers, and two of just about everything else. It doesn't take a genius to figure out that some people have to go.

This tumultuous atmosphere raises a number of obvious questions:

1.   How can I protect my job if my company is taken over by someone else?

2.   How can I read the signals regarding my future with a company that has been acquired?

3.   How can I prepare myself to lose my job in such a situation?

4.   Are there advantages that I might seek to exploit where mergers and takeovers have become a fact of life?

One good thing has come out of the chaos of our merger mania, and that's the fact that being unemployed no longer automatically carries with it a stigma. No one looks askance at people who don't hang in with one company for the gold watch. It's expected that people will hold a variety of positions thoughout their professional lives, not only because they choose to move more often, but because they will be laid off more than once. Today, it's estimated that nine out of every ten executives who are fired are victims of company mergers, acquisitions, or work force reductions. Being out of work is no longer something to be ashamed of. You're in good company.

How can you turn this situation to your advantage?

There's an old saying, "Necessity is the mother of invention." That's probably true philosophically, but men and women who live by it in their working lives are headed for trouble. When your company is acquired— and you're fired—is not the time to begin thinking about getting another job. People expecting success in this world had better start operating from the basic assumption that they will have to look for another job at some point in their careers, whether they want to or not.

An absolute necessity is to be constantly on the lookout for signs of when your job is in jeopardy, whether it results from a merger or acquisition or just general circumstances.

Have you found yourself being cut out of major projects that you would have been involved with before?

Has your boss, who usually communicates with you orally, started putting everything in writing? If so, it could be because he or she is building a file to be used to justify firing you.

Has some of your work been shunted to someone else? Has the easy rapport you've always had with your boss and colleagues become strained and less friendly?

You may be reading the signals wrong. Maybe your position is rock-solid, and you've allowed paranoia to sneak into your psyche. Then again, maybe you *are* about to be fired. As they say, just because you're paranoid doesn't mean you don't have enemies.

Be ready to be fired, even in the best days of your job. Keep up your personal personnel file, noting every achievement in your present job—how you contributed to the efficiency of your department, cut costs, increased profits, brought in a new client. A good résumé must show accomplishments. Don't rely on your memory after years on your present job.

In another chapter I mentioned the need to maintain an up-to-date networking list. If you haven't done it on an ongoing basis, you'll end up in the same position as the person who suddenly must come up with a sterling ré-sumé. The Boy Scout motto has always been "Be prepared." That motto ought to extend to every working man and woman in America.

How do you know your job might evaporate when talk of your company's being taken over becomes common knowledge? Rule number one: Assume it will. This, of course, leads into a whole debate over whether my call for a return to loyalty, and urging you to consider staying where you are, is at odds with this advice. I don't think there is a conflict in these two philosophies. Being prepared to look for another job doesn't mean you must put that preparedness into action. So long as you're receiving a paycheck from your employer, you owe the loyalty I spoke of. But the concept of an employer's demonstrating enduring loyalty toward its employees is a thing of the past. The company's management is looking for the best possible financial deal in a takeover or merger. It won't eliminate your job until that becomes a reality, but the *company* prepares for that eventuality, and so should you. This doesn't mean sending out résumés, making appointments with headhunters, and answering ads in newspapers. It does mean that if those moves become necessary, you're ready.

A question I posed earlier was whether there were aspects of the situation that could be exploited. I think there are. Because many companies entering into bankruptcy do it with the full expectation that they will emerge sound and in even better shape than they were before, individuals who can help bring about that turnaround have a shot at rising more rapidly than in a job with a more stable organization. I've seen many people come back from a job interview and say, "I don't want to work there. They're about to go into bankruptcy." Under ordinary circumstances I would agree with their assessment. But because the rules have changed dramatically and bankruptcy does not necessarily mean failure, jumping onto a sinking ship and helping to patch its holes can make instant heroes out of those who have the fortitude and personality to ride out a rocky voyage.

I remember receiving a call years ago from a company in Chapter 11 looking to hire a controller to help it through its financial woes. I said I'd try, and pulled out five résumés of highly qualified individuals, none of whom I thought would be interested in such a risky undertaking. I was wrong. Four of them eagerly went after the job, and one got it. Obviously, each perceived the challenge involved and, by extension, the potential for higher rewards than in a stable, prosperous company.

A few final thoughts on our bankruptcy, mergermanic industrial society.

I recently called a friend at home. His wife, who is employed at a major TV network that has recently been announcing massive cutbacks, answered. I asked, "How are you?" Her answer was "I'm still there!" That sums up the attitude of many workers in this crazy world.

Don't assume that after your company is merged with another and *you* are the one chosen to stay, everything will be clear sailing. Survivors often suffer interesting psychological problems. A number of studies have been done on the survivors of the Holocaust. Many of them seem to carry a sense of shame at having survived. That same phenomenon, in a much less dramatic way, of course, often creeps into the attitude of employees who survive massive cuts. In addition, the fact that the company for which you work had no compunction about firing good, capable, and long-term employees must naturally raise the question with you, a survivor, of how long you'll be allowed to stay.

Various surveys indicate that in the first year there is as much as a 20 percent increase in emotional problems of employees who survive a merger or takeover. In addition, almost half of all managers who survive are gone within the first year of new management.

The management of some companies that take over others are decent and honest. Executives will sit down with employees and say, "Some of you won't be here a year from now." That's a fair warning, and allows everyone to gear up to making a change. On the other hand, there are those who take over companies and say, "No one here has to worry. We're committed to keeping everyone employed." The next day, they start firing. The former is to be respected; the latter is to be distrusted. In either case, make sure your résumé is up-to-date, your networking list is complete and active, and your eyes are open to new opportunities.

The climate in which everyone must seek better jobs bears no resemblance to what it was two decades ago. This poses great difficulties for men or women seeking secure and better jobs. At the same time, for those who acknowledge this tenuous business climate and prepare for it, it can create potentials for success that are perhaps greater than ever.

As a nation, we now spend more on mergers than the combined expenditures for all research-and-development and new investment. Our companies demand more work from fewer people in an attempt to compete with aggressive and creative foreign competition. There are fewer jobs to be had, and they are more difficult to find.

To put the increased competition for jobs in perspective, consider the emergence of women in the workplace, including those qualified to hold middle- and high-level jobs. They represent a vast army of people who twenty years ago were not serious contenders for most of these executive positions. Add to them the growing number of older men and women coming back into the workplace, and the number of people competing for *your* better job becomes evident. Recognize these factors as you look for a better job. Accept the challenge they present, and take whatever steps are necessary to overcome them.

Some of those steps are covered in the next chapter.

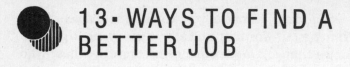

13 · WAYS TO FIND A BETTER JOB

Get your CART rolling

THERE ARE REALLY ONLY FOUR BASIC METHODS of searching for a better job. Put them together and they spell CART.

The *C* stands for *contacts*.

Although the world has gotten crazy, networking is still the best way, in general, to find a better job. It involves all the activities that result in contacts (remember, there's no luck involved)—things like hoofing it, making your career needs known to friends and relatives, keeping in touch and on good terms with past and present colleagues, bosses, teachers, professors, deans, the clergy, political parties, fraternal and business organizations. To be truly effective, networking has to be pursued with diligence and with a sense of organization. Remember, too, that networking is a two-way street. Be cooperative and offer, when appropriate, to be part of the other person's network. Again, a favor begets a favor.

An up-to-date phone and address book is essential; when you've decided to look for a better job, or need to find one because you're out of work, is not time to decide to update your phone book. It should be done on a regular basis. The few minutes it takes each day or week are well worth it.

It's tough to suddenly call on the people in your network for help in finding a better job when you haven't had any contact with them in years. Sometimes this rule can be broken, depending upon the nature of your relationship, but it's much better to keep in periodic touch, particularly with business colleagues. Some of the most successful people I know do this by noting items in newspapers and magazines that they think would be of interest to an individual, clipping them, attaching a very brief note (which need say nothing more than "Thought you'd be interested in this"), and mailing it off. An occasional phone call to keep in touch is always in order, as is making it a point to attend business and professional meetings at which you're likely to bump into some of the people on your networking list. And make sure you send to your network greeting cards on appropriate holidays, and anniversary and birthday cards if you know them well enough. I've always been interested in photography, and I routinely send snapshots to people, ones currently taken, or those from years ago that I run across in my files.

Many people, especially those who suddenly are unemployed, make the mistake of calling people on their networking list and asking if they have any jobs available. This puts the person on the spot and creates an awkward situation. Chances are there won't be a job open at the precise moment of your call, and the best anyone can expect from this approach is "We have nothing now, but I'll keep you in mind and get back to you if something comes up." Of course, that "promise" will be forgotten in a day.

A much better approach is to call people on your networking list and either ask for advice about finding a job or ask if they would be willing to act as a reference for you. People are always flattered when asked to give advice, and being considered important enough to function as a reference is flattering, too. Of course, you'd have to have had either some direct business dealing with anyone you'd ask to be a reference, or a personal friendship with someone who is well known in the business community.

What happens when you make these calls and take this approach is that you haven't asked anything of these people that is difficult to deliver—like a job. But you've gotten the point across that you are available, because you're unemployed or are interested in making a job change if the right one comes along. Once you've done this, it pays to follow up occasionally with a short note, or any other unobtrusive way of keeping in touch.

It's important also to remain visible to your professional colleagues in ways that don't involve direct contact. By seeking out opportunities to write for professional journals, you're assured of having your name, to say nothing of your good thoughts, placed on the desks and in the briefcases of many people who could prove helpful to you throughout your entire career.

Too many people I know arbitrarily narrow down the list of people they'll let know that they are looking for a better job or are out of work. I've never been able to figure this out, unless, of course, it comes from embarrassment, or just plain laziness. Selecting fewer people means having to make fewer calls and write fewer letters. The successful people I know take exactly the opposite tack. Each day they keep their eyes open for ways to expand their network, rather than narrowing it. The only reason I can possibly think of to be judicious in choosing members of your network would be to preserve the confidentiality of your job quest. But this doesn't come into play until you've decided to actively look for a job. That's really the whole point—nurturing and expanding your network when you *aren't* looking for a job means that your list will be long, current, and useful when you *are* looking for one. And, by the way, your network comes in very handy if you ever decide to launch your own business. Those people with whom you've networked may well become your first, even best customers or clients.

Don't make the mistake of restricting your active networking list to only those "big shots" who sit in lofty management positions and are assumed to be the best ones to help you climb your success ladder. By all means keep in touch with them if you have a legitimate reason for doing so, but nurture, with the same enthusiasm, those currently working on a level with you in your industry or profession, as well as those in lesser jobs. *Anyone* can be the source of information about a good job opening.

There is a secondary type of network that each person should develop and maintain. It consists of companies with which you have no connection—you know no one inside them—but that might have use for someone with your experience and skills.

Read the business section of your local newspaper and trade magazines in your field to get a handle on which companies are expanding. They may not be looking to fill jobs at the moment, but an expanding company generally will need to bolster its staff with good people. If your network is big enough and good enough, you undoubtedly will know someone on it who will, in turn, know someone in that expanding company whom you could contact.

Read the business pages of even your smallest local newspapers. Often, weekly newspapers give prominent space to local men and women who have been promoted. These executives on the rise might be looking to bring in new people, and you have nothing to lose by shooting off a résumé and letter to them.

You might also do a little thinking about changing industries, provided that would not represent too dramatic a loss of the skills and knowledge you've managed to obtain over the years of your working life. For example, a successful MBA financial analyst who decides in midstream to become a medical doctor (I know one who did) is going to lose a lot of ground for a period of time (but, understanding and accepting that, should make the change anyway if it is truly important). My acquaintance was successful, and was our family doctor until he moved to another area of the country.

More typical, however, is an accountant I know who, after ten successful years, felt he could not go much further in his field. He became very depressed about this until I suggested that there were many other areas of business that could benefit from someone of his caliber and knowledge. It took him awhile to accept this notion. When he did, and put his mind to it, he identified a number of possibilities in which his accounting background would stand him in good stead, yet would not constitute his only function. He incorporated his own personal interests and hobbies into his analysis of the situation. He'd become fascinated with computers, and was known as a whiz with the PC he had in his home. He conducted an aggressive job search and was hired by a software company that was in the early stages of developing a program for the accounting field, which would have to be marketed aggressively once its development was completed. My friend, the accountant, had significant input into the software program, and eventually headed up its marketing drive. He was happy from the first day he started in that new job, feels he has achieved far greater success than he ever would have had he stayed strictly in the accounting field, and is looking forward to even greater success in the future.

For some of your contacts, a note will accomplish more than a phone call. It's a matter of judging the tenor of your relationship with that person.

No matter how you go about it, the first and most successful way to find a better job, crazy world or not, is to have developed an extensive network and to use it effectively.

The *A* in CART is *advertising*.

People do find jobs through the help-wanted ads in their newspapers and trade journals. They should definitely be a part of the unemployed job seeker's plan. There are, however, some problems with ads that limit their effectiveness in some cases. Here they are:

Once a help-wanted ad appears, it can result in hundreds of responses. Some simple arithmetic will indicate that your chances of landing that job diminish in direct proportion to the number of people going after it. You can also count on whatever résumé and letter you send being screened by an assistant in the personnel department (or human resources department; some use both terms, some haven't changed department designation). Bear in mind that a function of a personnel or human resources department is to screen out those candidates who should *not* be considered for the job, as opposed to the person who will actually supervise the new employee, whose views might be quite different from those of personnel.

When answering an ad from a newspaper or trade journal, make sure your résumé and covering letter are top-notch, or they won't serve to move you up and out of the pack. If the ad presents a job that you are really interested in, and you feel confident that your credentials and experience will make you attractive to the employer, send your résumé and letter by messenger or by air courier. At least this will gain the employer's attention.

The problem with the way most people answer news-paper ads is that they send in their résumé and cover letter, make careful notes about which ad was answered and when, and then forget about it. That's a mistake. Once you've replied to the ad and have given it a decent amount of time—perhaps a week at the most—you must follow up. I recommend a phone call at this point, if it was not a blind ad. If it was a blind ad, send another letter asking about when you might expect a response to your résumé and requesting the opportunity to be interviewed for the position. Include another copy of your résumé with the follow-up letter.

A technique that I recommend when you run across an advertisement for a job that seems perfect for you is to rewrite your résumé specifically for that job, telling the truth, of course, but using more space for the areas you wish to emphasize and less space for items that aren't directly relevant. Also, clip the ad and attach it to the cover letter if you conform to at least 75 percent of what has been asked for. If not, leave out the clipping.

You should answer most help-wanted ads within a week if you fit the job perfectly. A high percentage of people wait more than a week to crank out their response to an ad. Some never send it because they assume it's too late. It's never too late, although a prompt reply is, of course, best. If you don't fit the job perfectly, I suggest waiting two or three weeks to answer the ad. This way you might stand a better chance because your letter and résumé have arrived after the initial flood of responses and thus will be seen and read carefully. Your hope in this case, of course, is that the employer has not been pleased with those who answered quickly and appeared to fit the job.

The people who place help-wanted ads—companies and recruiters alike—have their own special jargon. Anyone seeking a better job should read the ads carefully and frequently enough to become familiar with the meaning of job descriptions, titles, etc. Also bear in mind that job descriptions in ads often do not accurately indicate the credentials and experience actually needed for that particular job. If you don't match up precisely to the specs, but feel that what you can bring to that job is roughly in the ball park, by all means respond. Some companies want a PhD with twenty years of experience, but state that they are willing to pay only $25,000. They soon see that they are not likely to find someone with those credentials for that money, and adjust their requirements. That's why going in for the interview and impressing them can pay off in a good job, even though requirements are greater and your credentials less than what's asked for in the ad.

Beware of the "blind ad." These are ads in which only a post office box number is included instead of the company name. The dangers of responding to such an ad should be obvious. Your own company—your own boss, for that matter—may have placed the ad to see who in the company is loyal and who isn't. Your boss may have decided, without informing you, that he intends to hire someone to work alongside you in a similar job. Or a friend of your boss's may have placed the ad and, after receiving your letter and résumé, lets your boss know that one of his employees is looking around.

I know someone who worked at a small company for a few years, then saw an ad in the Sunday newspaper for someone to do roughly the same job for an association that represented that industry. She applied. A few days later her boss called her into his office and said quietly, "I have your résumé in front of me. I'm on the board of directors of that association. It's a small world, isn't it?" Of course it is, and she should have realized that possibility. She was fired!

There's a reasonably safe way for you, even though you are employed, to respond to blind ads, and that's getting a friend to answer them on your behalf, without disclosing your name. I call this a third-party response. It's certainly not as effective as a traditional response, but it is a lot safer. Have your friend write on his or her business letterhead.

Another approach you might consider is to try to guess which company placed the advertisement. You can often narrow down the possibilities by analyzing which companies in the geographical area stated in the ad seem to fit the job description by size or by a niche of the industry if it's mentioned in the ad. Then send a letter—not a résumé—without mentioning your present affiliation. In the letter, give the salient highlights of your background. Keep it to one sheet, with wide margins and adequate space between the paragraphs. Address the letter to the person or persons whom you expect you might end up working for. Often, you can find the name by calling each of the companies on your list and asking the telephone operator for the name of, let's say, the corporate controller, if the ad indicated an opening for an assistant controller.

People often wonder whether placing a "situation wanted" ad in newspapers and trade magazines will enhance their possibility of finding a better job. You're not likely to get a better job this way, but it has been known to work. If you're interested in living and working out of town, it may be a useful option to run your box-number ad in local papers, or it may just be used as another way of conducting a strictly confidential job search. Keep in mind, however, that if someone does want to interview you, you may have to travel at your own expense. The same holds true when *answering* an ad from an out-of-town newspaper.

As I mentioned earlier, answering help-wanted ads does get people jobs. I just feel, however, that the potential problems they cause *employed* people, added to the mass-appeal aspect of them, should make you think twice before responding to ads not placed by reliable personnel recruiters. Still, help-wanted ads should definitely be an adjunct tool in your search if you happen to be unemployed.

One final note on ads: research over the years indicates that as much as 75 percent of jobs are never advertised in the papers. That's one of the values of using a professional recruiter, the *R* of our job-hunting CART.

As the world becomes crazier, industry is, in general, focusing more attention on the quality of people it hires, particularly in jobs of great responsibility. It's about time. Because I've been in the employment field since 1948, I'm naturally interested in how businesses approach the hiring process. It has always been a source of constant amazement to me how many companies, who scrutinize every budget and product design with infinite care, approach the hiring of *people*—their greatest asset—like a young husband grocery shopping for the first time and grabbing any attractive box off the shelf, instead of reading the ingredients and checking the price.

As I say, it's getting better. It had to get better. This intensely competitive world has forced many businesses to cut back on staff, which means, of course, that those who remain must do more and better work. In order to find these top individuals, companies more than ever are turning to personnel recruiters, who, by nature of what they do, have access to the best available talent.

Enter the age of the *specialized* personnel recruiter. One hallmark of this crazy world is the intense specialization that has developed in virtually every field. At last count, there were at least three separate types of surgeons who operate on three different areas of the human eye. While many attorneys still function as generalists, more and more of them have moved into specialized areas of the law. I don't point to this as a negative; obviously, a skilled surgeon or attorney who spends his or her every day working on a specific part of the body, or in one segment of our complex legal system, is probably better equipped to handle that specialty. We benefit from it.

In the personnel recruiting field, the same stress on specialization has become increasingly important, and for the same reasons. There will always be the need for a general employment agency that handles a variety of jobs, usually lower-level ones, but today the needs of business for highly specialized and trained individuals have prompted more of them to deal with personnel specialists when trying to fill jobs. This is not to say that generalists in the personnel recruiting field do not fill many jobs calling for specialized skills. It stands to reason, however, that a personnel recruiting specialist, who focuses on only a few specialties, will have access to a larger pool of highly qualified men and women.

In the case of the company I founded, Robert Half International—which pioneered specialization in the personnel recruiting field—I chose to fill jobs for only financial and data processing positions. Being a CPA influenced me, of course, and because we have established a reputation in this area, those qualified individuals seeking better jobs in the financial and data processing fields naturally come to us. This means we have a large selection of skilled professionals to offer clients. The same holds true for all specialties, and a number of fine specialized personnel recruiters exist to fill these needs.

The point is that you, seeking a better job in this

ever-changing world, are better served by taking your special talents and experience to a recruiter who is able to match you, and your package of attributes, with a company looking for exactly what it is you have to offer.

Like everything else, all personnel recruiters are not the same. I began this book talking about ethics. One of the reasons was that when I started my company, the employment services industry was full of unethical operators. Fortunately, that has changed, although some still exist, just as there exist unethical companies and individuals in all endeavors. If you decide to use the services of a recruiter in search of a better job for yourself, be just as conscientious about choosing one as I preach every employer should be when hiring a new employee. Beware the high-pressure sales approach. That's not the job of a good, skilled, and ethical recruiter. If the personnel recruiter you choose is well known and respected, companies will turn to it when they need a good person with specific skills, which may mean more job possibilities available to you. Another reason companies turn to a respected and prominent personnel services organization is that they know the best candidates will be available to them. That's what it's all about.

Make sure any recruiter you choose has been around awhile and enjoys a good reputation. Fancy offices and a prestigious address mean little. I presume you will check out any company you may be interested in working for with great care, and urge you to do so. The same philosophy should hold true when choosing recruiters. After all, your career is at stake.

The final letter in our CART, *T,* stands for *temporary.* It has been my experience that many temporary positions turn into permanent ones. Over the years, our Accountemps division—which specializes in providing temporary financial, data processing, and bookkeeping help—has had thousands of its temporary employees hired permanently by companies at which they had worked as temps.

If you are between jobs, taking on temp assignments brings you into contact with a wide array of employers. What better way for an employer to judge someone than to watch that person at work every day for a week or two, or even longer? Hiring someone represents a great unknown to employers, no matter how diligent they've been in evaluating a résumé, asking probing questions during an interview, and checking references. A temporary worker who has been on the job quickly becomes a known entity. If that person gets along well with others, exhibits spark and willingness to work hard, and demonstrates in a hands-on way that he or she really knows the job, it makes great sense for an employer to tap that person to fill a permanent job opening, rather than going through the process of finding someone from outside. In a sense, this situation equates with my suggestion earlier that those looking for a better job should look first at the place at which they're currently employed. Most employers would rather promote from within than have to take a chance with a new person.

We even went one step further with our Executive Corner, the part of Accountemps that provides executive-caliber temporary personnel for such jobs as controller, chief financial officer, credit and tax manager, and MIS and data processing manager. Many of these professionals also find excellent permanent job opportunities by taking the temporary-service route. When a company sees a good professional working effectively on a temporary assignment, this individual will often get an offer to join the firm on a permanent basis.

An increasing number of highly skilled and experienced professionals choose temporary work not because they are between jobs, but because they prefer the freedom it gives them. This is a growing trend in our society. According to a survey by the National Association of Temporary Services, technical, industrial, and medical temporaries represented 37 percent of the 5 million workers who filled temp jobs. And the numbers are growing every year.

High-tech temps are increasing at a rate of between 300 and 500 percent a year. We now see temporary services with names like Rent-a-Chemist. Companies increasingly go outside for services and products. Seventy percent of the value of one of the major automobile manufacturers' vehicles is subcontracted.

In a study by The Conference Board, 25 percent of the American work force (25 million of us) are "contingent workers." Thirty-three percent of all retail employees are part-timers.

The age of the specialized temporary worker is with us. Take advantage of it.

As I said before, employers often hire temporary workers for good permanent positions after the workers have demonstrated the ability to do the job. Employers feel it's safer taking this approach than hiring an unknown quantity.

Using the same reasoning, keep in touch with your former employers (provided, of course, that you left them on good terms). Here again, that employer knows you. If the company was sorry to see you go, and currently has an opening, you'll be seriously considered for it.

That's our job-seeking CART. I like to imagine the visual of an enterprising and career-oriented person getting on this CART, skillfully steering it through this crazy world, and parking it in front of the company that has offered a truly better job.

Reminders on Ways to Go After a Better Job

≡ Maintain and upgrade your network.

≡ Learn how to read the ads.

≡ Go after jobs even if your background and experience don't match up exactly to what's specified.

≡ Don't answer blind ads.

≡ Use the services of specialized recruiters, but choose carefully.

≡ Do temporary work when you are between full-time jobs.

≡ Be active in trade and civic associations, and write articles for your industry's trade publications.

14 · WHEN TO LOOK

I look for jobs only on sunny Mondays

MANY PEOPLE SEEKING A BETTER JOB DEVELOP A keenly honed ability to rationalize why they haven't found one yet. The reason, of course, never lies within them. It always has to do with externals.

I've known a number of people who are convinced they've analyzed the right times to go after a better job. One in particular had a theory that the only two days of the week to look for a job were Monday and Tuesday. "The end of the week is always dead," he told me with a straight face.

His theory was that because most jobs are advertised by personnel recruiters and companies in the Sunday papers, you had to be there no later than Tuesday. After that, all the jobs had been gobbled up, and you wasted carfare, shoe leather, and time making the rounds on the final three days of the week.

The fact is that most jobs are not advertised, and those that are in the Sunday papers were probably written on Wednesday and turned in to the newspapers on Thursday for their Sunday editions. I urged my friend to consider the leg up he would have by being in contact with a personnel recruiter or company toward the end of

97

the week, when they're getting ready to submit ads for new job openings to the newspapers. He didn't seem to appreciate my logic, and the last time I spoke with him he was still in the same job and bemoaning the lousy job market out there.

Some job seekers avoid looking for a new and better position on days when the weather is bad. They postulate that on such days interviewers are generally depressed. If the weather is really bad, they go on to say, interviewers are rushed because many of their staff have stayed home. Think of the dilemma job seekers face if they believe in looking for work only on Monday or Tuesday, and in fair weather. If snow happens to fall on those two days, that wipes out an entire week.

So far as I'm concerned, the best possible day to look for a job is Monday through Friday, preferably on those days when the weather is at its worst. On those days, all the fair-weather job hunters are huddled up at home, which translates into less competition for you.

Not only that, showing up for a job interview on a rotten day says something very positive about you, the sort of thing that employers are always seeking. It says that you're a person who's really interested in the job, who isn't afraid to go out in bad weather (which means you'll take fewer days off than those individuals who never venture out unless the sun is shining). It says to an employer that you're a person who, by nature, works hard and doesn't allow adversity—climatic or otherwise —to get in the way of accomplishing what you've set out to do.

This tendency on the part of some people to limit their chances of finding a better job because of faulty preconceived notions extends to all aspects of life. I once met a salesman who had to rank as one of the leading failures in his industry. We talked about his lack of success, and he explained to me what had caused it. (Allow me to exaggerate a bit to make my point.)

There was no sense calling on customers in January, because everyone was weary after the holidays. In February the weather kept most customers out of their offices. March was a transition month; the long winter was over, and they simply weren't in a buying mood.

We all know what's wrong with trying to sell anything in April. The IRS occupies everyone's minds throughout the month. I was pleased to hear from him that May was generally pretty good, except that more and more people were beginning to plan for summer vacations, which distracted them from his sales pitch. All the buyers were attending their kids' graduations in June, and everyone is on vacation in July and August, so why bother trying to call them?

September wouldn't be a bad month for a salesman except that's when families are driving their kids to college. Clearly, October was the prime month for any salesman to make his mark. The problem was that when this individual tried to get through the door in October, no one knew him because he hadn't been there all year.

November? That means Thanksgiving. December? Here we go into that holiday season again, when no one is interested in buying anything except holiday gifts.

That same approach actually represents the way some job seekers think. They don't bother looking for work in December because of the holidays. They avoid the summer months because those in a position to hire are on vacation. Besides, it's hot and sticky and you walk into the interview not looking your best. Better to wait until October—provided, of course, that people in your industry are hiring in October.

And so it goes.

If you're unemployed, looking for a job is a full-time

occupation. At least, it should be. If you were working in a job, you would be there Monday through Friday, from at least nine until five. Seeking a better job should command even more time and effort—including nights and weekends. The more time and effort you expend, the better your odds are for success. More leads are produced, which translates into more opportunities from which to select.

If you're seeking a better job from the more secure base of being employed, you obviously can't devote your full energies to it. You can, however, apply the same diligent effort as though you were creating your own business on the side.

In either case, you are engaged in the selling of a product—*you!* That product has usefulness twelve months a year, but if you pick and choose the times you'll go out and market it, you'll soon find that your share of the market is pretty skimpy.

15 · RELOCATING

Company must be within walking distance
of my home

I'VE SEEN MORE THAN ONE RÉSUMÉ DURING MY
career that included a line like the above. I've seen résumés that restrict any employment to a company that is
within walking distance of favorite restaurants. I've seen
résumés with a demand for a private parking space, or for
space to be provided in the office for a motor scooter.

Obviously, people who include this kind of restriction
on a résumé are going to have a tough time finding a
better job—or *any* job, for that matter.

For men and women seeking to build a career base,
being flexible in terms of *where* they will work is extremely important, especially in the early stages of a career. More large companies are relocating people these
days, and employees who are reluctant to make a move
because of personal considerations severely handicap
their potential.

The highly respected trade magazine *Personnel Journal* has surveyed its subscribers over the years regarding
trends in employee relocation. Three years ago, 57 percent of the respondents indicated that during the preced-
ing twelve months their companies had relocated
employees. Last year that figure was up to 61 percent.

According to the survey, not only are more companies relocating their people, they're spending more money on it. In the same period, the amount of money spent on employee relocation increased from $2.9 billion to $4 billion, a 38 percent increase during a period when cost-of-living increases were small and interest rates favorable.

I've heard two theories expressed by employees who've been asked to relocate by their companies. One is that by accepting the challenge of a move, and by being given additional responsibility in a field office, your star rises in the eyes of management back at headquarters.

The other theory is that the farther away you are from the center of power, the less likely your chances of success with that company—the out-of-sight, out-of-mind philosophy.

When job opportunities are plentiful for employees whose skills are in demand, I suppose such people can afford to analyze a request to relocate and be picky in making their decision.

Anyone seeking a better job has to put *flexibility* near the top of his or her priorities. A number of young people approach their careers backward. Some want the things now that previous generations knew would come later, once a solid career base had been laid. Some choose where and how to live based upon individual preferences, rather than accepting the fact that the place to live during the formative stage of a career should be where the best jobs are.

Obviously, there are legitimate personal reasons for declining to relocate, but I urge anyone called upon to make such a decision in this tumultuous business climate to be sure his or her reasons are valid and compelling.

Having to decide whether to relocate because your employer asks you to is one thing. Making a decision on your own to relocate in search of a better job or, if unemployed, to find a replacement for the one you've lost is another matter. In either case, you are not going against the wishes of a company. Instead, you are making a career decision that involves not only seeking a job but weighing the risks involved. The question also must be answered whether you're looking to make a move in search of a better job, or simply because you wish to live somewhere else. Either reason has merit, but make sure you understand your motivation and goal before setting out to achieve it.

If a better job is what you're after, you won't exclude too many geographic areas in which to seek it, at least not because of personal living preference. Obviously, there are areas of the country where the industry in which you've gained your experience is stronger than in other locations. For instance, if your expertise and background is in insurance, Hartford, Connecticut, would be a logical place to look. At least that was the case a few years ago.

Don't indicate on your résumé areas of the country to which you will or will not relocate. I once received a résumé from a young man who indicated he would relocate anywhere except Vietnam, North Korea, Libya, Iran, and New York City. I suppose he was making a point, although I don't think his résumé was the place to do it.

Once you've picked your spots (and this is under the assumption that you're seeking a better job, not choosing a location because of personal preference), I suggest you contact a business service in the city of your choice, use its local box number address and phone number, and arrange to have it answer your calls. Have a letterhead made up with that local contact on it. Many companies are reluctant even to respond to a résumé and letter from someone out of town on the assumption that it will involve expense on their part, as well as a certain amount of inconvenience. Having an address and phone number in such a company's area at least precludes being ruled out from the start. In short, do anything to give yourself the appearance of being from that city, rather than seeking employment from thousands of miles away.

Subscribe to the leading local newspapers, especially on the days of the week when employment advertising is heaviest. Be quick to follow up on any ads that appear suitable for you. Subscribe to your regional edition of the *Wall Street Journal*, and keep your eyes peeled for jobs in trade journals that serve your industry.

Respond immediately to any company that reacts to your résumé and letter, and mention during the first few minutes of the telephone conversation that you do *not* live in that city, that you established an address and phone number there because you felt it would be more convenient and expedient, and that if there appears to be the potential of your working for the company, you expect to pay all your own expenses. You may hope that this does not become necessary—and in many cases an interested company will bring you out for an interview at its expense—but don't put that burden on the company. If you're going to seek employment out of your area, come to grips with the reality that it's going to cost you money.

Try to turn the initial telephone contact into an informal interview. Obviously, no company is going to hire you based upon a telephone conversation, but how you come off during it will determine, to a great extent, whether you're asked to finance the next step. Read and reread chapter 21, on interviewing, and approach a telephone interview with exactly the same spirit and preparation as if you were going into the offices of the company.

Consider running an ad in the city's best newspaper, using your mail and phone drop as a way to contact you.

Your best route to finding employment out of town is through a personnel recruiting firm. Obviously, those with a strong national (and perhaps international) network of offices can be of most help. Go to the branch in your current city and ask about job opportunities elsewhere. Some recruiters do not have many offices around the country, but work with affiliates. Choose those firms that have a solid reputation and have been around awhile.

You can also find the names of local recruiting firms in the city to which you wish to move. Practice the same caution in making your selection as you do in your home city.

Sometimes someone seeking employment from out of town stands a better chance than a job seeker who lives next door to the company. Such candidates are more appealing simply because they are from someplace else. This thinking runs parallel to what has always annoyed employees in corporations when their suggestions are ignored but an outside consultant is brought in, gives the same suggestions, and is applauded for them. The old definition applies here: "An expert is an S.O.B. from out of town."

Employers tend to make a quicker decision when it involves someone from another city or town. If it's a company in a smaller town, there is a tendency to have heightened respect for people with "big city" experience. And some companies like to hire from outside the area to avoid "inbreeding."

If you are hired by an out-of-town company, you also enjoy the advantage of being less likely to be fired or laid off. Companies are reluctant to dismiss a person who has gone through the turmoil of having moved there for the job.

Obviously, there are risks in making a move. If you relocate to a small town and lose your job, the employment opportunities are significantly less than if it had happened to you in a big city. If you've been in that small town for a while and have put down new roots, the thought of relocating again can be traumatic. Your initial relocation might have been wonderful, especially because you did it of your own volition. *Having* to do it again isn't nearly as palatable.

If you're sincerely seeking a better job, maintain flexibility and don't rule out any possibilities, whether it's in an area of employment that you hadn't thought of before or in a city that you'd never considered moving to. Good job opportunities pop up in the strangest places, and at the strangest times in our lives. Keep your eyes open for them and, in the spirit of a highly mobile military unit, be prepared to move fast.

16 · LEAVE NO STONE UNTURNED

When you try many things, some things will work

WHEN YOU'RE LOOKING FOR A JOB, YOU'RE DOING a bit of detective work. Networking, for example, is detective work because you're seeking clues to viable job leads. My advice to job seekers anxious to find a better position is to do everything fast and at the same time, like any good detective.

Remember, your detective work will lead you down many blind alleys before you come across even one workable job lead. In the recruiting profession, job leads for specific candidates fall under the heading *research*. As you seek better job opportunities, you, too, are involved in research, which, after all, is what a private detective actually does.

Let's assume, for example, that you spot an ad in the *Wall Street Journal* that reads something like this:

CHIEF FINANCIAL OFFICER

A publicly held consumer electronics manufacturer located in one of the largest cities in Nebraska and doing a volume of $300 million requires a bright, energetic, and talented CPA, MBA with a great deal of experience as a CFO in our industry. Salary range in low six figures with a comprehensive fringe package. Respond to Box ZZ 004, Wall Street Journal.

Understand, this is a blind ad, with no way to identify the advertiser—unless you do a little detective work.

There aren't many large cities in Nebraska, and there certainly aren't many consumer electronics manufacturers in that state doing $300 million in sales, so it should be easy to identify the advertiser. Your stockbroker may be able to pinpoint it. Dun & Bradstreet, Standard & Poors, or a regional directory available in the library are all good sources of information that could lead to an identification. You may not be able to isolate it, but you certainly should be able to narrow down the possibilities to two or three, and if you're lucky (or not so lucky, depending upon how you view it), you could come up with a dozen possibilities. Then again, in other circumstances—when the company is located in, let's say, the Boston or Los Angeles area—you might not be able to identify it at all. But because you've adopted the role of detective while seeking a better job, you're not at all discouraged when leads turn out to be red herrings. You're willing to view each tiny piece of information as potentially leading to the solution—in this case, the landing of a better job. In other words, by doing everything you possibly can to uncover that job, you increase the chances of having some things work.

Let's assume you're convinced that there are two companies in Nebraska that could have placed that ad. What do you do about it?

First, go back to your network and try to find someone who knows an individual in either of those companies, preferably someone in a decision-making capacity. If the contact does, perhaps you can persuade him or her to call the Nebraska contact and ask if they could use a CFO with strong experience in their industry—not letting on, of course, that the ad has prompted the inquiry.

If you can't find someone who's a handshake away from the right person, you should write a letter to a top management man or woman at both firms and ask whether there are any openings for someone with your background and experience. These letters are commonly known in our industry as "broadcast letters," although in this case the word *broadcast* really does not apply. In this case, it's more of a customized letter prompted by a specific ad.

Under no condition should you mention that you saw an ad that might have been written by that company. You will, of course, tailor your résumé and cover letter to meet the requirements stated in the ad.

Using the example of the Nebraska electronics company I created, you would highlight your experience as a chief financial officer with a publicly traded consumer electronics manufacturer. You would also indicate that you are a CPA and an MBA, if that's the truth. If you're not an MBA, simply leave it off your letter and résumé. Make sure you end your letter by asking for an appointment.

Even if your research did not reveal the name of the company that placed the ad, so what? It's possible that one of the other companies receiving your credentials might be so intrigued that they decide to call you in for an interview. In this case, your letter fell into the broadcast category, and worked.

I have had close friends confide to me that they have used private investigators to help track down job leads. When I first heard about this approach I thought it was, to be honest, off-the-wall. It then occurred to me that it might make sense for high-level executives looking for leads to top jobs. It certainly costs a lot to engage the services of a quality private investigator, but if the prize is big enough, it's probably worth it. Actually, when you consider the cost of some counseling firms that "groom" job seekers by teaching them to prepare their résumés, provide source material for a direct mail campaign, and give advice—some good, some not so good—the cost of hiring a private investigator to work specifically for you in finding realistic job possibilities might make sense. I really don't know to what extent this approach is used, but it's something to think about, particularly if you're currently employed.

Years ago I knew someone who left an excellent job to become CFO of a mid-sized manufacturing company. After a year, he was asked to falsify certain SEC documents. He refused and was fired. Later he learned that the two principals in the company had criminal backgrounds. Had he investigated the company and its officers, he would have discovered this and not made the move.

I always urge that people who've been offered jobs do whatever reference checking they can on the company. For someone leaving a lucrative and secure position, this is a must; a private investigator can be well worth the money.

The most effective job seekers train themselves to be on the lookout constantly for clues to where the better jobs are, and use creative techniques to get an interview. The more you think about good approaches, the more leads and interviews you'll come up with. The more leads and interviews you have, the better your chances of landing the kind of job you've been seeking.

17·HOW TO DRESS

When in Rome...don't wear green

WITH YOUR CART (CHAPTER 13) FIRMLY IN PLACE, it's time to take the next step in seeking a better job. However, there's something else you should think seriously about so you don't put your CART before the horse.

One of the fallouts of the recent past among those who believe in "doing your own thing" has been an unnecessarily strident focus on ignoring how we dress. The problem is that the concept that people should be judged by what they are, rather than how they look, has great validity, and it represents the sort of human values we all should treasure.

However, while the worth of a man or woman is not represented by clothes, the *reality* in business is that how you dress—how you look to others—plays a vital role in how far you'll advance. Like it or not, take it or leave it, that's the way it is, and for those seriously looking for a better job, it had better be heeded.

The minute we meet people, our instant reaction to them is formed by what we see, long before we have a chance to explore how they think. That is especially true for someone meeting a potential employer for the first time. It holds just as true in a person's present employment, where, I urged earlier, you should always dress a little better than your colleagues, and view each day as a job interview within your present company, or a day in which you'll be called upon to give a spur-of-the-moment presentation to the chairman of the board. So when I talk about dressing right for a job interview, I intend for it to apply to your current job as well.

There are, of course, professions and jobs in which clothing means little, or where deviating substantially from the norm is acceptable, even encouraged. Creative people who work in advertising agencies often tend to embrace trendy clothing, which is acceptable in the atmosphere of agencies. People who work in the fields of fashion design, the theater, art galleries, and other artistic endeavors have the same kind of freedom in their choice of clothes and, by extension, hairstyles and makeup.

But for most men and women seeking greater success and better jobs, American business, large and small, has its acceptable "uniform." It doesn't say that you must wear blue, or brown, or gray; it *does* say that yellow suits and pink shoes will necessarily work against you.

Throughout this book I stress the need to improve your *odds* of getting a better job. If you walk into a prospective employer's office and light up a cigarette, even though there is an ashtray on the desk, you have, perhaps, significantly cut your chances of getting that job. If you go to lunch with that same person and order two martinis in this age of light drinking, you may have done the same harm to yourself.

Clothing is just as important, as are personal grooming, hairstyles, use of makeup, and the decorative objects you choose to wear. It may offend you that you will be judged to a great extent upon how you look, but then you had better be willing to settle for jobs that don't necessarily represent "better."

People invest in businesses. For the job seeker, the

business is *you*, and you should be willing not only to invest some money in you—in *your* business—but to acknowledge that if you don't have a good sense of what clothing is appropriate, you should seek advice from someone who does. Or, better yet, look in magazines like *M* or *Working Woman* and see what they're showing for working people. Just be careful to stay away from the mod, trendy styles. Play it safe; stick with traditional clothing.

The uniform of American business has not changed in decades, and is unlikely to change in the near future. It is based upon conservative clothing values, and demands certain adherence to basic rules of color and style. Those who conduct business in the mainstream of American economic culture are comfortable with each other because they are dressed similarly.

An artist friend of mine, who provides graphic art to a number of leading corporations on a free-lance basis, knows that he could go to meetings with corporate leaders dressed in the style of the artist that he is. He never does. He wears a conservative suit, white shirt, and tie to those meetings because, as he says, "I believe in fitting comfortably into the milieu in which I'm functioning at that moment." This artist is, obviously, a believer in the old adage "When in Rome, do as the Romans do." He's playing it smart. He's improving his chances of getting the assignment he's after, which is, after all, the reason he bothered to go to that meeting in the first place. He's astute enough to realize that making a statement about himself by wearing clothing that is different from that of those with whom he's meeting is, at best, a childish exercise—unless, of course, there is such a psychological payoff to making such statements of individuality that getting the assignment is secondary. If you fall into that latter catagory, you probably should stop reading this book and turn to a fashion magazine instead.

I've heard people complain over the years that their career success has been stymied because they insist upon being their "own person." "If employers don't accept me for what I am, they'll just have to do without me."

I applaud them for their convictions. I also have little sympathy for their lack of career advancement. No one forces anyone to dress a certain way in this country, which is one of its precious attributes. Along with that freedom, however, comes a parallel understanding that complaining about failure because you chose to exercise your freedom at inappropriate moments is wrong.

An objection many people have to those of us who urge maintaining a proper wardrobe is that it costs money. That really doesn't stand up to scrutiny. I am certainly not suggesting that to succeed in business one must maintain an extensive and expensive wardrobe. It isn't a matter of size or cost; rather, it is choosing the right clothing, minimal as it may be, to accomplish the goal of getting a better job. A young man starting out does not need six suits. What he does need are two suits of the proper colors and style, along with enough shirts to be able to wear a clean, unfrayed one every day and some conservative ties that can be changed, along with the color of the shirts, to give his two suits a different look each morning. The same philosophy holds true for a woman seeking a better job. There may be many frilly, avant-garde dresses that appeal to an individual woman, but they will do nothing to enhance her possibility of gaining greater success in the American business world. Women, too, are playing it safe.

Basics!

Like everything else, dressing properly for business involves basics. Stick to the basics and you won't have to worry about whether you're dressed wrong for an interview with a company that's offering the kind of job you want.

An analogy is deciding what to wear to a party. Obviously, the best way is to find out the mode of dress for the evening and dress accordingly. But many times we don't have that input. The answer? Dress up. You may be out of place with your suit and tie when everyone else is wearing jeans, but you certainly would be more out of place in your jeans when everyone is wearing dark suits and ties.

What represents basic and correct clothing in today's business climate?

For a man, it's suits in conservative shades of blue and gray, suits that are well tailored, do not involved patterns that are unusual, and are kept cleaned and pressed. You can never go wrong with shirts that are white or blue and do not contain patterns. Simplicity. Basics.

Ties with tropical sunsets on them may be fun to wear to a masquerade ball, but are out of sync in the workplace. Even though you buy your suits and shirts in outlets, I recommend that you invest in a couple of expensive ties. Muted, solid colors, rep patterns, or subtle stripes are all acceptable, but resist the temptation to buy a flashy tie that catches your eye in the store. Or, if you are absolutely obsessed with buying that tie, wear it on the weekend.

Women should follow the same philosophy I recommend for men. Avoid wild patterns, flashy dresses, suits, and accessories. Stay away from the over-made-up look. Your hair should be nicely styled, but not in an exteme fashion, such as hair dyed in unnatural colors. And, by all means, don't use too much perfume. Stay away from the low neckline, and the length of your skirts and dresses should generally be in the range of what is in vogue—but not the extremely long or extremely short look.

That brings up a good point. No one suggests that you must live a life of conformity seven days a week. What you do on your off-hours is your business and, unless it brings you into contact with business-related interests, should remain exactly that—your business. We all have virtually limitless opportunities to express our individuality in our clothing, lifestyle, and personal interests, but those aspects of our lives should be kept in that context.

A word of caution here, however, about viewing your off-hours as a time when anything goes in the way you dress. Lounging around your own house is one thing, but going out into the neighborhood, especially to gatherings where a number of people at their leisure will be congregating, should not be viewed with such a cavalier attitude. You never know when you will meet someone who, if not in a position to give you a better job immediately, might become an important part of your overall network of contacts. How you dress, how you look to that person, will determine, to some extent, his or her reaction to you. The simple fact is that we form initial opinions about people based primarily on how they look. Yes, weekends might be a time for causal dress, but always bear in mind that you're constantly being interviewed in this life. That's why I advocate going to work each day with the attitude that you're being sized up—being interviewed—for the possibility of advancement in the firm. You don't have to go to the same extremes during your off-time, but I wouldn't go too far afield, either.

If you want to get a better job in this crazy world, accept the fact that you must dress accordingly.

There are many people who don't argue with this, and who want to dress correctly for the jobs they seek or to impress superiors in the jobs they currently hold. They find it impossible, however, to choose clothing that meets that goal. For example, a man might go to a clothing store, see a suit that is "dark," and, without carefully examining the material or style, buy it. When he wears it to work, will he notice that it may be made from cheap material, have strange-looking dark lines through it, and be further embellished with gold threads? For the same money, that man could have bought a basic gray or blue suit that, while not representing Savile Row, is appropriate for the day's business.

One thing to keep in mind when buying a suit for business, especially if your wardrobe is limited, is to choose fabrics that are wrinkle-resistant. You certainly don't want to drive an hour to an interview and arrive wearing a suit that looks as though you slept in it. When determining whether a suit is sufficiently resistant to wrinkling, crumple the sleeve with your hand. If it doesn't snap back pretty much to its original shape, don't buy it.

I always advocate that when writing a résumé, people who are unsure about their grammatical and spelling skills seek the advice of someone who is comfortable with those things. Evidently, most people don't bother, because I receive thousands of résumés a year that confirm this. The same principle holds true when choosing clothing for business. Acknowledge that you do not have a good eye for it, and seek the advice and active help of someone who does. There's nothing embarrassing about that. If you have a friend or family member who is obviously successful in the mainstream of American business, and who seems to dress properly for it, ask that person to go with you when you shop. It isn't necessary to go to a high-priced clothing store. We are a nation of factory outlets; these places offer a wide selection of clothing at low prices, and with someone accompanying you who understands the way you *should look*, you can walk away without breaking your budget, and with the kind of clothing that is always appropriate.

Don't trust a salesperson to give you the proper advice. By the same token, don't rely only on your spouse to select your apparel, unless he or she has a proven track record in choosing the right clothes for business.

Take the time and interest to evaluate your wardrobe on a continuing basis, just as you would your investments. Your closet contains an important investment. What's in it will determine, to a significant extent, how well you do throughout your career. Keep your clothes in good order, especially if you have few of them. Keep track of what you wear each day, and what shirt and tie you wear with a given suit, or scarf with a dress. Be always on the lookout for sales through which you can replenish items in your wardrobe that have seen better days. As I've often said, looking for a job *is* a job, and everything that contributes to it should receive your serious attention.

No matter what you choose to wear in the way of suits, shirts, ties, and dresses, it is inexcusable for anyone seeking greater success in business to be unkempt, and to allow his or her clothing to be less than neat and clean.

What image is presented by a job seeker who comes to an interview with shoes that are scuffed? Obviously, keeping shoes shined does not take money, aside from the cost of a can of polish and a brush. Those of us in the personnel services industry see it every day: ties with stains on them, frayed collars, unpressed suits, socks that fall down around the ankle bone, dresses that no longer fit, dirty fingernails, smeared lipstick, body odor, hair in the same position it was when the alarm clock went off— all giving the distinct message that these individuals do not care enough about the jobs they're seeking to come into the interview neatly groomed and properly dressed.

If you're the sort of person who cannot abide the conformity I'm suggesting here, think of it this way: if you're dressed inappropriately, and have not paid particular attention to your grooming and hygiene, you create a situation in which *you* must be uncomfortable. Remember my comment about public speakers who have a button dangling or a spot on their shirt or blouse? You owe it to *yourself* not only to be dressed in a manner that is appropriate to the company and position you're seeking, but to give yourself the advantage of at least knowing that the way you look is correct. If you know that, you are then free to express your ideas, to sell yourself based upon your credentials, experience, and knowledge—to present to the interviewer the *real* you that we treasure in this society.

If you have unruly hair, take the time and spend the money with a barber or hairdresser who knows how to tame it.

Get some expert advice on what hairstyle is most complimentary to you. Don't trust your own judgment; most of us have trouble seeing the real us in a mirror.

If there is some obvious and distracting feature, consider plastic surgery. I'm a person who believes that most plastic surgery is frivolous and only feeds an overly heightened vanity of the recipient. On the other hand, if there is part of you that genuinely gets in the way of your being confident, there is nothing wrong with seeking the services of a competent plastic surgeon who can correct what you perceive as a defect. That same defect may mean nothing to someone else. If it hangs you up, seek a solution. As I've often said, this is not a dress rehearsal for your life. This *is* the only life you've been given.

Looking right—dressing right—says one thing about each of us. It says we take pride in who we are and how we present ourselves to the world. To a prospective employer, the communication of that pride means a great deal. A person exhibiting concern about outward appearance is likely to be perceived as having the same concern for the jobs he or she is called upon to perform. If I have taken the time and paid attention to how I present myself to a prospective employer, it may be assumed that I will pay the same attention to how I look when I am to meet with an important client.

People seeking better employment in their own firm, or with another, must be prepared to look their best at all times, even at the end of a long day.

If your days are full with a succession of interviews, consider carrying a "survival kit." You may want to convert part of your attaché case into an overnight bag. Include in it a comb, brush, nail file, razor, makeup, mouthwash, some small paper cups, after-shave lotion, a mild perfume, deodorant, a few wash-and-wipes, perhaps a washcloth, some disposable shoeshine polish, a toothbrush, toothpaste, and anything else that will help you spruce up when it comes time for an important interview. Get to the interview early and use the rest room for freshening up.

Check the weather forecast before you leave the house in the morning. If there's a possibility of rain, take a lightweight raincoat that fits into your attaché case and/or a small folding umbrella. That may seem axiomatic, but all you have to do is look around on a busy city street on a rainy day to see how many people don't prepare for the weather. There's nothing worse than running into an interview wearing a drenched suit and apologizing for the water you're dripping on the floor. If nothing else, it indicates that you're not someone who plans ahead.

If you're the type who insists upon doing your own thing, do it. But do it on your own time, or be ready to accept the negative consequence in the business world.

Years ago, someone related to me a story that had great meaning to that person; the story makes a useful point here.

This person was driving along in a car on which he was having trouble making payments. He'd come from a long day at the office. It was hot; he couldn't wait to get out of his suit, which he wore only because he knew it was an appropriate suit for the business he was in.

He saw a hitchhiker in the distance. He drew closer, and saw that the hitchhiker was a young man with very long hair, who obviously carried on his back all of his possessions. The man in the car had an immediate reaction: "He's got the right idea. He's a free spirit."

Then, as the driver passed the hitchhiker, he glanced in the rear-view mirror and saw the hitchhiker make an obscene gesture because he hadn't been picked up.

The moral to the driver was clear. The young man was saying, "Let me do my own thing, in my own way, but give me a ride."

We can't have it all ways. Getting a better job in this world, crazy or not, involves analyzing what's expected of us, both in performance and in the way we dress and present ourselves. If you really want a better job, do in Rome as the Romans do during the period of time in which you're employed, and vent your creative styles of dress or lifestyle on your own time.

A final note on dress for business. According to John Molloy, who wrote the definitive book on the subject, *Dress for Success, never* wear a green suit. I'm not sure why this is so, but his advice has always been worth listening to.

Reminders on Appearance

≡ First impressions are based upon the way you look.

≡ Learn how to dress properly. Don't leave it to chance.

≡ Your business is *you*. Invest in yourself. Look right.

≡ Be "your own person" on your own time when it comes to fashion.

≡ Dressing right doesn't mean a big wardrobe, but choose carefully.

≡ Stick to basics. Lean toward the conservative side.

≡ Avoid excessive jewelry and makeup.

≡ Skip the fashion fads.

≡ Take the advice of friends who know what proper business fashion is.

≡ Keep all clothing clean and pressed.

≡ Create a small kit of personal items and include it in your briefcase when going for job interviews.

18· WRITING YOUR RÉSUMÉ

Who needs a résumé anyway?

THE MOST OBVIOUS REASON TO HAVE A WELL-prepared résumé is that it might be required to get you an interview or, in some cases, will be requested of you at the interview.

But there are other reasons for having a good résumé on hand that you might not have thought of.

The actual act of writing a résumé gives an assessment of your advantages to an employer, as well as giving you a self-analysis of your disadvantages. The résumé is nothing more than an ad for you, and good ads never reveal negatives. When appropriate, your shortcomings can be discussed at the interview, but it's always inappropriate to expound on them in a résumé.

Keeping your résumé up-to-date while you are employed gives you clues as to how to present yourself to your current employer when asking for a raise, a promotion, or both. Obviously, you won't show your résumé to your employer when requesting these things, but you can use it as a reminder of your accomplishments since last talking with your boss about bettering your situation.

If you're going after a new job and a résumé isn't required, the very fact that you've prepared one can function as a blueprint for you when preparing for the interview. In the sometimes tense atmosphere of a job interview, we tend to forget those things that might sell us. Having a good résumé to constantly go over, including just before going in for the interview, can help avoid this.

At the same time, your résumé will, if properly and honestly done, point out to you your failings. By being aware of them, you can get yourself ready to answer questions that focus on those aspects of your background and experience. And, of course, it also gives you an opportunity to strengthen areas of weakness after you've identified them to yourself—with the help of your résumé.

Judging from the thousands of poorly written, ill-conceived, and in many cases downright silly résumés that have ended up in my "Résumania" file, there are lots of people who would be better off not using a résumé at all.

On the other hand, those who learn how to prepare a proper résumé will have taken a solid step forward in finding a better job. A good résumé won't get anyone a job; a poor one surely loses jobs for lots of people.

There are easy ways to come up with a résumé. You can buy any one of dozens of books that present samples of "good résumés" to their readers. You can go to a résumé preparation service and have it create one for you.

I counsel against both approaches, which is why you will not find a sample résumé in this chapter.

The problem in having someone else—the author of a book or a person working for a résumé mill—prepare a résumé for you is that it comes out looking exactly as though someone else has done it. Those carbon-copy résumés flood the desks of people who hire. They have almost identical formats, take the same approach, and in too many cases even use the same words. How, I ask, can people find better jobs if they choose to place themselves on the heap of cookie-cutter résumés? Better jobs are gotten by people who set themselves apart from the pack, and who rise above the mountain of résumés because they've caught the eye of a person who will take them to the next plateau of consideration.

Most people approach the writing of a résumé with grave trepidation. It represents *writing* to them, a task they avoid with the same fervor as when called upon to write a letter to a friend. They have been sold a myth that writing takes a particular God-given talent, and that because they don't possess this talent they are always destined to come up with bad résumés.

The fact is that a résumé is not a writing exercise in pursuit of a Nobel Prize in literature. In fact, those who approach it that way create résumés that may end up in my "Résumania" file. (I should mention that I have been collecting unusual, amusing, and bizarre résumés for years, and present some of the best of them each month in my "Résumania" column in Dow Jones's *National Business Employment Weekly*.)

A résumé should be an accurate representation of what you have accomplished in your life as it applies to employment, and should indicate to a prospective employer what you can bring to that company. It is nothing more than that. The problem is that because most people don't maintain that personal personnel file I've urged you to adopt in earlier chapters of this book, their résumé does not accomplish that.

A résumé should begin with your name and indicate a way to reach you should an employer be interested. Sound overly simplistic? It sounds that way to me too, but I've seen many résumés that do not include a telephone number, and in some cases don't even include an address. This "how to get hold of me" beginning portion of a résumé should not include silly restrictions on when or how to reach you.

"Please do not call before ten. My mother sleeps late." That's an actual item from a résumé one of our offices received.

Keep it simple: name, address, and telephone number.

Most résumé mills and advice books suggest beginning a résumé with "Job Objective." I generally disagree with them. By stating a job objective, you potentially rule yourself out of being considered for other jobs in that same company, jobs that do not match precisely with the objective you've stated. Remember, being flexible when seeking a better job opens up far more opportunities. If you've presented your education and work experience in a cohesive and understandable fashion, the sort of jobs for which you're qualified will be self-evident to the person reading it. Skip "Job Objective" on your résumé unless you pinpoint your purposes. Then you might need three or four résumés, each prepared with basic honesty, but beefing up those aspects of your background that have direct applicability to each job you might be qualified for. A better place to indicate areas of particular interest is in the letter that accompanies the résumé. We'll get to that later.

There are basically two types of résumé. One is *functional*, the other *chronological*.

For most people who have had a relatively continuous track of employment, the chronological approach makes the most sense. It should begin with your most recent employment, which, hopefully, is ongoing. If it isn't, too many out-of-work job seekers seem compelled to indicate the reason they are not currently employed. I wouldn't do that. Nothing is to be gained, and much is to be lost.

Here are a few of hundreds of "reasons for leaving" from résumés in my files:

"Married my boss."

"I never had one job longer than six months due to emotional instability and being in trouble with the law. I moved quite frequently."

"My employer and his wife were murdered."

"Want to live near the sea."

"Boss was a sadist."

"My boss was nice in the morning, but after drinking his lunch he was unbearable."

"Fired, fired, fired."

"Quit, quit, quit."

There is no reason to indicate why you left any job listed on your résumé. That can be covered during the course of an interview. Listing reasons for no longer being employed, however sensible they may be, only comes off as apologetic or, in many cases, smacks of sour grapes.

At the same time, don't fudge with your employment record. Don't say that you are still employed at a company if you're not. That brings up the whole question of honesty on résumés, a subject that I've delved into at great length over my career.

Most people do lie on their résumés to some degree. Some people get away with it, particularly at lower-level jobs. Most people don't get away with it over the long run, and the job offers that go down the drain once references are checked are legion. That doesn't mean you should take pains to point out your inadequacies. What you should do on your résumé is paint an accurate picture of your background, highlighting the positive aspects of it and downplaying the negative aspects—without lying.

The problem with most résumés, even if they are carefully prepared, is that they end up listing employment, positions, and responsibilities without ever indicating the potential value of the résumé writer to a new employer. There is no inherent appeal in simply laying out the companies for whom you've worked and the job titles you held at those companies. Did you make any significant contributions to that company, the sort of contributions that you can bring with you to your new employer? There's that personal personnel file again coming to the surface. If you were the manager of quality control for seven years at the XYZ Company, be sure to indicate in that section of your résumé that by eliminating two screws and one nut in the manufacturing process, you not only created a better product, you saved the company $600,000. That's the kind of information an employer sits up and takes notice of. The same principle can be applied to any job. Again, I'm not suggesting that you embellish your accomplishments. That will backfire on you when your previous employer is asked about it. Few of us go through our working lives without making some positive contribution to the company or department in which we work. Keep a record of those contributions, document them, and highlight them on your résumé.

There's always debate about how long a résumé should be. Most counselors like to say, "Keep it to one page." That's bad advice. A résumé, like a novel, should be as long as it needs to be to make its point effectively.

Too many people fill their résumés with so much trivia that it goes on for pages and obviously is too long. Others, who buy the notion that a résumé should be kept to one page, frequently fail to fully explain their contributions and accomplishments, and shortchange themselves in the process.

If you've been employed for a long time, there is no need to lengthen your résumé with descriptions of the jobs you held while in high school and college. On the other hand, if you're someone starting out in the working world, those jobs will at least indicate to a prospective employer your industriousness, and that even though you are young, you have had experience in the workplace.

Most résumés contain a section on education. Those people who did not complete higher education often are tempted to try to cloud that fact by the use of vague language. People who read a lot of résumés have become savvy where this is concerned, and pick it up immediately. Be honest; don't claim to have graduated from an institution if you haven't. Don't hesitate to indicate courses you've taken that bear upon the job you're going after, but don't overplay it. If you've been working for a long time, your education becomes less important. Again, for people just starting out, education plays a much more vital role in judging job candidates. Put everything in perspective on your résumé. If your educational background is impressive, by all means give it in detail. If it isn't, deal with what you have in a succinct manner and get on with the rest of it.

People who have been active in a number of professional and civic organizations usually list them on their résumés, as they should. This kind of involvement outside of working hours is always impressive, and if you haven't been active in that regard, I suggest you correct that deficiency, not only because it will give you something positive to put on your résumé, but also because it furthers your professional knowledge and results in the sort of expanding network that's important throughout a career.

If you've been published in professional journals, by all means list those publications. If you've received awards, those belong on your résumé, too. But be realistic in evaluating those items. If they're marginal and have little or no bearing on your professional credentials, leave them off. A padded résumé is immediately obvious to most people reading it. Keep everything solid; you can always embellish in a cover letter, and during the interview.

A good percentage of the résumé items that end up in my "Résumania" files come from under the heading "Personal." There is really no reason to include personal items on any résumé, unless they have direct bearing upon your occupation. Here are some examples of personal items that I've collected from résumés around the country:

"My wife and I really like each other."

"Present home is a modern four-bedroom on 1/3 acre, conveniently located to good schools, shopping, and churches."

"We have a pregnant dachshund named Abercrombie, and no children."

"Can't roller skate."

"Have weakness in the toes."

"Thirty-three years old, one daughter, age nine, currently entering bankruptcy proceedings."

"Married with no children, no house, and no furniture."

Get the point? Discuss personal things—maybe—during the interview. They don't belong on your résumé.

We've come a long way in the area of anti-discrimination in employment. Still, many people include material on their résumés that would not only be illegal for an employer to ask, but that creates a preconditioned negative response to their quest for employment. There is no need to include on your résumé your age, your religion, your national origin, your marital status, or your health. The old adage "We are our own worst enemies" is proven true time and time again on résumés. What's even worse is that people will include that sort of material on their résumés and then explain it. "I am sixty-three years old, but my friends all tell me how energetic I am." Or "I may be a woman but I am not hung up on fem-lib. I am willing to make coffee."

I suppose the reason for so many ridiculous items on résumés is that we tend to be insecure, and this crazy world has done nothing to alleviate that. The most rational of men and women become irrational creatures when faced with writing a résumé. Don't let that happen to you. It's tough enough finding a better job without sabotaging your chances on the piece of paper that represents your initial presentation of yourself to new employers.

Some thoughts now about references:

References should not be listed on the résumé itself. If an employer shows interest in you, you should provide that person with a neatly typed list of people to contact. Have this list made up in advance and be sure to include the correct spelling of each person's name, including middle initial, correct title, full address, and telephone number. Also, take note of how the company prefers to be addressed. If the Widget Corp. does not capitalize the "t" on "the," and prefers *Corp.* to *Inc.*, follow its lead. In the case of Robert Half International Inc., there is no comma between *International* and *Inc.* This was deliberate, and I'm never impressed when someone writes and includes a comma.

Don't, however, include anyone on your list of references who hasn't been contacted personally by you and given permission to use him or her. In fact, because job seekers should do everything possible to improve their odds by anticipating every potential hitch in the job-hunting process, I suggest you "prep" your references to whatever extent possible. It depends, of course, on the relationship you have with them, but because you've chosen these individuals, you obviously are on good terms with them. (Maybe I shouldn't be so certain about that.

Years ago, I was about to hire a mailroom clerk. He gave his mother as his only reference. I called her, and she said, "Maybe if he gets a good job he'll straighten out.")

It pays to give those former employers whom you've chosen as references a copy of the résumé that has been submitted to your prospective new employers. Discuss the résumé with your references; you might have included an item that doesn't match up with the way one of them remembers things. Straighten out those differences before that item is raised by the person who has interviewed you, who might come away with the feeling that you've stretched the truth.

At the same time, it's worth your while to draw up a list of all the potential questions that you anticipate being asked during your interview. Supply to your references the general sort of answers you'll be giving. For instance, the interviewer might ask you how long you worked at a former job. If your answer is six years, let that particular reference know that you'll be using that number. It really isn't fair to expect an employer of many years ago to recall with total accuracy the details of your employment, especially if this is someone who has moved on. Of course, the personnel department of your previous employers won't have much trouble in resurrecting details. It's also possible that your recollection about certain events and specifics is faulty. Better to be in sync with your reference than to have such discrepancies emerge during a reference check.

You might be asked why you left a former job, whether you got along well with your co-workers, whether you left on good terms. By advising your reference of the answers you'll give to these questions (and assuming he or she agrees with your answers), you've taken yet another step toward improving your odds of being hired.

Be selective when supplying a list of references. Make sure the employer is sincerely interested in you before you hand it out. If references are called too many times, they tend to become apathetic and less enthusiastic, might even be annoyed at a large number of intrusions into their working day.

When choosing a reference, make sure you settle on those people who are likely to give you an enthusiastic one. A reference given for reference's sake will do nothing to advance your cause.

A standard line on the bottom of résumés is "references available upon request." I recommend leaving that line off. It accomplishes nothing; any employer assumes there will be references to check. By including it, you add an unnecessary line that only diverts attention from the most important part of your résumé—your achievements.

I've been writing up to this point about the chronological résumé, something that most people are comfortable with and that suits their needs. For some, however, the functional résumé is more effective.

A functional résumé should be used by anyone who has long gaps in his or her employment history, or someone looking to change careers. A housewife looking to enter the workplace after years of raising children obviously cannot list a long chronology of job experience. In that case, it's better to focus on what work experience has existed, no matter how far in the past, and to highlight skills and knowledge rather than a list of one so-called better job after another.

Hiring professionals are skilled, however, at picking up those functional résumés written by people who have to take that approach because their employment record is spotty and/or filled with gaps that reflect unfavorably upon them. A functional résumé does not begin with the name of a company and the dates employed. It starts with skills and knowledge, and the firms with whom those skills and knowledge might have been gained is secondary. Dates are not important in a functional résumé. People who have been gainfully employed for many years, but are looking to make a dramatic change in their careers, often use a combination of the chronological and functional résumés. If an accountant who has spent fifteen years in his profession wishes to become a taxidermist, his accounting experience has little impact upon his chances of finding a job in a new and unrelated profession. If, however, that same accountant has been practicing taxidermy as a hobby for years, he can weave that information into a résumé that also indicates his solid work record in the profession he wishes to leave.

If you use a functional résumé, keep in mind that it, by its very nature, often raises doubts in the minds of employers about whether something is being hidden. That's why it's vitally important that the material on it be straightforward, clearly indicating what you've done with your life. For the housewife looking to reenter the workplace, a functional résumé should indicate that you devoted a number of years to raising your children. You can also touch upon the volunteer work you did that has applicability to the job you're seeking. The same for college courses you took, free-lance work you performed, and anything else that enhances your credentials to the person who is reading your résumé, and who must judge whether you're someone worth hiring.

The question of how a résumé should look physically is often brought up. It should be appealing to the eye, with enough white space to render the printed portions readable. If the material that you feel you must put on your résumé goes into two pages, better to do that than to crowd it all into one page that presents a gray image to the reader. Leave spaces between major sections. Have sufficient room on either margin in which people can make notes. Above all, be sure that it is neatly typed using a fresh ribbon, and on a good typewriter that is in decent repair. Better yet, have it professionally typed.

Many job seekers, particularly those fresh out of college, go to print shops where they have their résumés typeset. That gives the look and feeling of having come out of the sort of résumé mill I've referred to.

Creating and producing résumés is a time-consuming task. It's worth it, however, and I recommend going beyond simply creating one perfect résumé. As I said before, I don't believe in stating a job objective on a résumé unless that résumé is intended *only* for that purpose. That doesn't mean there won't be two or three positions that your background and education might qualify you for. Each of those potential areas of employment demands a separate résumé, and if you're serious about finding a better job, you'll take the extra time and effort to do this.

Let's say, for example, that your background has put you in touch with marketing, selling, and advertising. Obviously, many of those areas might provide a better job for you, but one résumé that attempts to cover all those bases lacks the necessary focus.

For such an individual, three specialized résumés should be created. One will emphasize the marketing aspects of the person's experience. The second will focus on sales background and accomplishments in selling. The third will have at the forefront the individual's advertising experience. When a marketing job opens up, the version of the résumé that highlights that aspect of the person's background will be sent. The same holds for potential jobs in sales and advertising. We can't be all things to all people, and shouldn't try to be on our résumés.

At the same time, a "general" résumé should be prepared in which the disparate major focuses of your experience are given equal weight. I suggest this because as companies trim staff, the role of a generalist is becoming increasingly important to many of them. If you sense that a job opening requires a jack-of-all-trades in the general area of your experience, use the all-encompassing résumé to go after it.

If you know of a very good job at a very good company, prepare a custom-made résumé for that job. It won't take too much time, because you'll be able to extract and adapt sections from your other résumés to use in this customized one.

I advocated earlier doing what you can to separate yourself from the pack of people applying for the same job. I suggested sending your résumé by Federal Express or by messenger in order for it to stand out.

That does not mean, however, that taking a dramatically different approach with your résumé itself is advised. I've seen résumés accompanied by photographs of the applicant lounging on a beach, driving a tank, or standing in front of a wall full of plaques that can't be read, and probably shouldn't be. I've seen résumés printed on paper six feet long. Some people choose to have their résumés prepared on garish green paper with white type, virtually impossible to read. Others include line drawings to illustrate various highlights of their career, or create banner headlines in large type.

These are not ways to gain the right kind of attention.

A résumé should be printed in clear black type on white or off-white rag paper. Yes, better-quality paper does make a difference. It should be of standard letter size, and should not include photographs or drawings. I also recommend spending the few extra cents on postage to send the résumé in a large envelope so that it remains flat, not folded. Not only does this give the employer a résumé that looks better and, by extension, is slightly easier to read, it stands out in the pile because most people will send their résumés in the smaller, number 10 envelope.

There are, of course, certain creative fields in which a "creative" approach can be effective. The problem here is that if your creativity isn't especially creative, you're certain to fail in your quest for that job. It's very much like someone who applies for a job that involves heavy writing and submits a résumé rife with grammatical and punctuation errors. For the résumé itself, I recommend sticking to the basics, and letting your accomplishments speak louder for you than any gimmicks you might come up with.

Every résumé should be accompanied by a letter. Unfortunately, some people see this as an opportunity to write six-, eight-, and even ten-page letters in which they tell a prospective employer more about themselves than the employer or, for that matter, anyone else would wish to know.

A cover letter should be brief and to the point. It should indicate interest in the position that is open, without going overboard. It should highlight some aspect of your background that has particular applicability to the position, and should, if appropriate, mention mutual friends or professional colleagues who might have encouraged you to apply for the job.

Résumés and cover letters represent you to a potential employer. If they aren't well written, correct in grammar and punctuation, and don't make sense, chances are you'll never even reach the second phase of your job search—an interview.

Everyone who prepares a résumé and cover letter, and who is unsure of his or her skills in basic writing, should seek the help of a friend or relative who has some background in this area. A résumé should be read by as many eyes as possible in search of typos, misspelled words, and awkward phrases. To simply dash off a résumé and cover letter and send it to an employer who is offering what appears to be a better job doesn't save time; it wastes time—yours! Every good writer will acknowledge needing a good editor, and that certainly holds true for the writers of résumés.

Reminders on Résumés

≡   A good résumé won't get you a job; a bad one will lose you plenty of them.

≡   Prepare your résumé yourself. Avoid résumé mills, from which every job candidate looks pretty much alike on paper.

≡   Include only pertinent information on your résumé. Generally skip "Job Objective"; always skip irrelevant personal items and silly demands. Keep it simple.

≡   Have other astute people read your résumé before sending it, especially someone with knowledge of clear, basic writing and the use of the English language.

≡   Use a chronological résumé, unless you've been out of the workplace for a long time.

≡   Don't indicate why you left previous jobs.

≡   Create your résumé from the personal personnel file you've been keeping.

≡ Don't include references on your résumé.

≡ Create a separate résumé for each area of strength in your background. Also, create one general résumé. And don't hesitate to create custom ones for special situations.

≡ Don't use colored paper or outlandish type styles. Stick to 8½-by-11, good-quality paper.

≡ Use your résumé to put yourself in the best possible light, but be honest.

19·FITTING IN

Be yourself, but...

I TALKED IN CHAPTER 17 ABOUT THE NEED TO conform where dress is concerned. I'd like to go a step further and suggest that you might even consider becoming a clone in the interest of finding a better job.

Whether you're offended or not by this concept will depend how deeply ingrained your "do my own thing" philosophy is. If the concept of conforming, of adapting in your job, upsets you, feel free to skip ahead to the next chapter.

On the other hand, if the reason you've bought this book is that you sincerely want to get the best job possible, you may find this chapter helpful.

I once worked in a company with a man who cloned the boss in almost every detail, including taking up the smoking of cigars, buying the same brand as the boss did, and using identical motions in lighting and holding them. He quickly became second-in-command of the company. Actually, he overcloned. His boss died, and he was soon out of work.

People rejoice in their own image. I recall a cartoon years ago in which an obese, ugly man was lying on the beach. He turned his head and saw another man approaching who looked like his twin. On this second man's arm was a beautiful blond wearing a skimpy bikini. The caption under the cartoon reflected the first man's thought: "Nice-looking couple."

If you're looking to improve yourself with your present company, take some time to analyze the style and behavior of the person who is in a position to do you the most good. If your boss is aloof and formal, inject a little of that into your own personal style. It doesn't mean you have to change your overall personality and approach to people. It's just a matter of adapting a little to what your boss obviously will respond to positively.

Do it with clothes. Choose your wardrobe with an eye toward matching up with your boss's preference in suits, or dresses.

Become familiar with your boss's extracurricular interests and hobbies, and develop at least enough knowledge of them so that you can be conversant on the subject. Take note of the way your boss deals with visitors and, when greeting your own visitors in the presence of your boss, adopt a few of his or her mannerisms, such as body language—never to the point of mimicking, of course, but just enough to indicate that you, too, include elements of that style in your greeting.

If your boss has an aversion to brown suits, and you're in a clothing store trying to decide between a brown and a blue suit, why not choose the blue one? If wearing brown suits is really important to you, buy both and save the brown one for weekend cocktail parties.

If you've decided to look for a better job outside your present employment, you can put the same philosophy into play. It's a little harder, of course, but it can be done. If you can find out about the style of the person who will be interviewing you, inject some of it into your presentation of yourself. Certainly, if you get through your initial interview and are called back for a second one, you will have had the opportunity to observe this person and can make minor adjustments then.

Let's not have any misunderstandings in this chapter. I am not advocating becoming a carbon copy of anyone else. People who try to do that always come off looking foolish, and are quickly recognized as shallow and transparent.

I'm not talking about changing the *substance* of you. But if you can establish a slight edge over other job candidates because there are certain aspects of you that naturally appeal to the person making the decision, that makes pragmatic sense to me.

20 · KEEPING YOUR JOB SEARCH SECRET

Who, me?

IF YOU'RE CURRENTLY UNEMPLOYED, YOUR BEST approach is to let as many people as possible know that you're looking for a job. If you're employed, however, a great deal more discretion must be practiced, for obvious reasons.

Looking for a job while holding a job is tricky, at best. You must be circumspect in the way you go about it or you may suddenly find yourself looking for a job as an unemployed person.

Employers seem to have a sixth sense when it comes to knowing that their employees are looking for another job. Sometimes an employee makes it easy. I remember one instance where a young woman used the office copying machine to run off multiple copies of a résumé. The machine jammed; the boss saw what was happening and fixed the jam, pulling from the machine's innards the first page of the résumé. It was, to say the least, embarrassing to that employee, if not downright fatal to her career opportunities with that company.

Some time ago I developed and published seven "clues" to help employers detect whether an employee was looking for another job. I based this on years of experience, as well as on some surveys done in this area, and did it as an aid to employers.

Those clues can be equally as valuable to you, an employee looking outside your company for a new and better job. These are the things you *shouldn't* be doing while conducting a surreptitious job search.

1.   If you usually take lunch hours of a certain duration, and suddenly begin extending them, the question naturally has to come up in your employer's mind whether you're using that time for interviews. The same holds true if you seldom take a day off and suddenly begin calling in sick.

2.   If you start receiving an unusual number of personal phone calls, an employer realizes they could be from your wife or husband who's been taking messages from recruiters, or from employers themselves.

3.   Employees who ordinarily communicate frequently and openly with management, and who suddenly stop that practice, could be trying to keep a low profile until they make their exit. Generally this occurs when an employee has gotten fairly close to taking another job.

4.   If you begin to dress a lot better than you usually do on the job, it's possible to assume that you're going out on an interview that day. Or if you dress better for a number of days, it could be because you're getting ready for interviews whenever they come up.

5.   Employees who start taking personal belongings home may have been offered a job and are getting ready to announce their departure.

6.   If you've always taken your vacations at the same time of the year and suddenly change that pattern, it could be because you're about to launch an intensive job

search, or want to get a vacation in before announcing you're leaving the firm.

7. Employees who have always taken an active and aggressive role in meetings and begin to sit back and limit their participation could be operating on the theory that they don't want to make waves before their departure.

Is it disloyal to look for another job on the sly while still employed? I don't think so. It's pretty much an accepted practice. Most companies, for that matter, will not inform you if they are seeking your replacement. It would be nice if they did—and some do, out of interest in an employee's well being but don't count on it. You have a right to pursue your career goals, and if you've determined that they're better served with another company, you are not being disloyal by pursuing them quietly and privately. You do, of course, have an obligation to your current employer to perform up to the standards expected of you until you actually do make a move. You have a further obligation not to steal your employer's time by using office phones, taking off paid work time for interviews, using copying machines, fax machines, and the like to pursue your job search.

Most employed people have a temptation to confide in at least one person in their organization that they are looking for another job. Usually it's someone who can be trusted, and there's a fair chance you'll be right. On the other hand, chances are even better that that person, well-meaning as he or she might be, will tell someone else "in confidence"—who will, in turn, tell someone else—and pretty soon lots of people know. I suppose there's a law to govern this; it never seems to fail. Be prudent! Keep your job search to yourself as much as possible, and confine the circle of people who know about it to as few individuals as possible.

Do *not* use your job search as leverage for improving your current position. How many times have we seen it happen? An employee takes a stand and says, "If this doesn't happen here, I'll have to find another job." More times than not, the response is "I think you'd better start looking." By the same token, don't look for another job to give you bargaining power in your current one. Here's what often occurs. An employee accepts another job, informs his or her boss, and hopes for a counteroffer. Many times, such a counteroffer is made. If that happens to you, my advice is not to accept it, and to go on to your new job. The minute you accept a counteroffer, you also must accept the fact that you may no longer be viewed as a loyal employee. Surveys indicate that you'll be gone in six months to a year anyway. Playing the counteroffer game is bad practice, and you're the one who generally will be hurt by it.

If you've really thought things out and firmly believe that you must seek employment elsewhere, be committed to that goal, pursue a new job with diligence, and, when it's time to announce your decision to leave, do it with the conviction that no matter what counteroffers might be made, you are leaving.

A growing trend these days is to have an employee who has been dismissed leave almost immediately, rather than linger, which might have an adverse effect upon other employees. This is especially prevalent in cases in which an employee has been fired, the theory being that it makes good sense to pay that person whatever severance is involved and have him or her leave rather than stay in a nonproductive status and, possibly, impact negatively upon the morale of others in the department.

For employees who have resigned, more often than not, the employer expects that they will stay for a decent period of time to help in the transition of the work to a new person. One way to score considerable points with an employer you are about to leave is to be instrumental in bringing in and training your successor. Be available to answer questions even after you leave. And be sure your attitude is healthy during your last weeks on the job, and after you leave it.

Don't gloat to your colleagues about your new position. It can do nothing but cause resentment with them. Work as hard during those remaining weeks as you did early in your employment with the company. In fact, give it some extra effort so that when you leave you're viewed in a positive sense, something that can help you considerably when that company is called upon to give you a reference for yet another job you're seeking. They might even contact you in the future with a fantastic offer to come back.

Be sure to follow up a verbal resignation with a short, very polite letter to your boss, with a copy to the personnel or human resources department; you can be sure it will go into their permanent files. Years later, when the company is contacted for a reference, someone in the personnel department can pull out your file and see by your letter that you left on good terms. Be sure to include in that letter only praise, no blame. Indicate how much you've enjoyed your time with the company and how much you've learned from the experience.

No matter what the circumstances are that have caused you to resign, never allow anger or resentment to surface. You may dislike your boss intensely, and be leaving because you can no longer tolerate working for that individual, but you have nothing to gain and everything to lose by venting those feelings. Be content with the inward satisfaction that you've found a better job for yourself, and use your final time in your present job to build a strong bridge back to it, rather than burning it.

21 · THE INTERVIEW

It'll just be a pleasant chat

I COVERED MANY OF THE RULES OF JOB INTER-
view conduct and etiquette in chapter 3. Let's talk now
about how we mentally approach an interview.

Some people go after jobs methodically, and use
every resource available to them. Then, when it's time for
the interview, they approach that critical phase of the
hiring process in a casual, almost offhand manner. They
view the interview as nothing more than a time when
someone will ask questions and they'll answer them.
Being relaxed when being interviewed for a job is good.
Going into an interview without having diligently prepared for it is not, and you diminish your chances of
turning it into the sort of success you're hoping for.

Comedians who are known as good ad-libbers work
hard ahead of time to come up with many of their suppos-
edly off-the-cuff brilliant asides.

I've been interviewed on hundreds of radio and television talk shows, and although I am very comfortable in
that situation, I would never think of going to one of those
programs without having done significant thinking, planning, and rehearsing.

Veterans of the talk-show circuit become skilled at

making sure that no matter what questions are asked, they are going to get across the crucial points *they* want to make and finesse the ones they can't answer—or prefer not to answer. Authors experienced at being interviewed determine in advance exactly what comments from them will help create interest in their books. Somehow they make sure these points are made. People seeking better jobs can take a lesson from this.

For me, those few minutes on the air represent an opportunity to offer helpful advice on employment and career tips, with which I am familiar, as well as to create an interest in the company I founded, and those aspects of that company that I wish to get across to potential clients and job candidates. In your case, it is an opportunity to sell yourself. If you fail to do that because the interviewer hasn't led you into areas in which you feel you can make your points, you've failed. It doesn't help after an interview to moan that the interviewer didn't pave the way for you to highlight your strong points. That's your responsibility, not the interviewer's.

The first image that comes to many people's minds when I suggest this approach is the typical politician being questioned on specific ideas and programs. It's infuriating the way they totally ignore what has been asked, and give canned speeches. That, however, has become so commonplace in the American fabric of political life that we tend to shrug our shoulders, smile, and ignore it.

You can't be as blatant as a politician in a job interview. You must weave selling points about yourself into the flow of the conversation in such a way that it appears that you have answered questions. In reality, you have used those questions as a launching pad for your own personal sell. This is where rehearsal comes in.

As we've all become aware, video has found a prominent place in almost every aspect of our lives. Job seekers are now sending out "video résumés" to prospective employers, occasionally with favorable results, but usually eliciting unfavorable reactions. There are courses offered all over America in which corporate executives are videotaped while making speeches and answering mock interviewer questions, and then have the opportunity to review and sharpen their performance. Athletes make good use of videotapes of their games, and learn much from what they see.

You can learn a great deal by conducting a mock interview in front of a video camera and analyzing the tape. Such video setups are available through employment counselors, and college placement services throughout the United States make use of them. If you don't have a video recorder, work with an audio tape recorder. Decent cassette tape recorders cost very little, and can be of tremendous help in enabling you to judge not only the content of your answers but the tone in which you deliver them.

Before any of this can be accomplished, there must be concerted effort on your part to anticipate every potential question, to formulate the right answer to each of them, and to practice working into your answers those points that, while they may not seem germane to the question, are made to sound as though they are.

The first time I ever appeared on television was a long time ago, in living black-and-white, on public TV in Portland, Oregon. It was a half-hour interview and, of course, because it was public television, there were no commercials. I was told that the interviewer, who happened to be a Russian prince who held two doctorates, was a mild-mannered, low-key host. He seemed that way upon my initial meeting with him. We settled into the studio on chairs facing each other. One camera behind me focused upon him, the one behind him on my face.

I was fully prepared to talk about subjects like hiring,

firing, getting a job, and all other aspects of the work-place. In fact, a couple of days before the show the host had called me and discussed the nature of the subjects he was interested in exploring during the interview.

I felt supremely confident and well prepared. Then, as the show began, the first comment out of the interviewer's mouth was, "Mr. Half, we both agree that almost all employment services are unethical."

I immediately assumed that the camera covering me was focused tight on my face, and I tried to keep an overall pleasant look and conceal my sudden nervousness and anger. I responded, "Mark, unquestionably there are some unethical employment services, just as there are some unethical doctors, lawyers, accountants, and radio hosts. But the overwhelming majority of people in our industry are very ethical, and try their best to fill positions. They even give a great deal of professional advice that they don't charge for."

Mark spent the next ten minutes grilling me on this inappropriate subject. Then, to my good fortune, he blundered. He started to make it clear that he believed in government control of all employment. At that point I broke into the conversation and said, "Mark, just a moment. What I hear you saying is that you approve of manpower control by the federal government. Are you aware that the first thing Hitler did was to control manpower, and one of the first things Castro did was to control manpower? I'm sure that's not your intention." Frankly, I believed it *was* his intention, but I didn't want to create an even more antagonistic atmosphere.

Suddenly, my host became a kinder and gentler interviewer, and he spent the rest of the show discussing exactly what I was prepared to discuss. I have to admit it was a traumatic way for me to get my feet wet doing talk shows. After that, I made sure that I was always prepared with contingency plans. Fortunately, in the countless radio and television interviews I've had over many years, I never had an experience that was as bad as that one in Portland.

Years ago the reigning king of late-night talk radio in New York was a gentleman named Long John Nebel. Nebel was known as a ruthless interviewer, although I didn't find him that way when he interviewed me. He had the ability to unsettle a guest and then get at information the guest would have preferred not to have broadcast. Nebel's skill in this had a great deal to do with his natural approach to asking questions. He also used a technique that few people knew about.

When a guest—particularly a controversial one—arrived at the studio a half hour before the show, that guest would be seated comfortably in a waiting room. The program's producer would pleasantly ask the guest to sign a standard release form. While the guest was reading the form, the producer would casually ask, "Is there any subject you'd rather not have brought up tonight?"

In most cases, the guest was pleased and relieved at this demonstration of sensitivity, and would mention some aspect of his or her life that would be embarrassing to have discussed over a radio show. What the guest didn't know was that the conversation with the producer was being picked up by a microphone. Nebel was sitting in his office listening to it.

You guessed it. Nebel would lead into the program in a pleasant and cooperative manner. Then, at an opportune time, he would bring up precisely the thing the guest had asked not be discussed.

I mention this because many people seeking better jobs end up being thrown during an interview by a question that they hadn't expected, and that they perhaps would have preferred not to have been asked. It's for that reason that I suggest that each person about to go to a job interview make a list of the ten questions that he or she absolutely would not want to have to answer. Once that list is drawn, every question on it should have an answer prepared with care and skill. With that out of the way, you can walk into an interview and not fear the unknown, because the "unexpected question" is now expected.

Also, in regard to questions, you should never assume that once a question is asked and you answer it, the interviewer will move on to another subject. In fact, almost every answer to a question will prompt follow-ups, to clarify or illustrate what you've said.

"Do you feel that you've exhibited superior leadership skills in the job you're in right now?"

"Yes, I think I have good leadership skills."

In most cases the question isn't going to stop there. The obvious follow-up is "Give me some examples."

Anticipate that this will happen with most questions, and have examples ready to back up every answer you give. Remember, the important word is *credibility*.

When analyzing the question you're likely to be asked, including those you don't want asked, use your own good sense in anticipating the follow-up questions that will also be put to you.

"What were the courses you enjoyed most in college?"

"I really enjoyed the sociology and psychology courses I took, because I think they apply to the marketing career I've been pursuing."

"Yes, that makes sense. What schools of psychology do you think have the most direct impact upon the marketing of goods in this society?"

Fumble time. If one of the points you wish to make is that you feel sociology and psychology play an important role in marketing, be prepared to discuss it further and in some depth.

Question: "What do you enjoy doing on your off-hours?"

"Well, I play tennis and I love to read."

"Really? What authors do you especially enjoy?"

I could list examples of follow-up questioning forever. The point is that when you anticipate a question, anticipate that there will be at least another on the same subject, and probably more. A favorite question is "Who has influenced you the most in your life?"

The most acceptable answer always was "My mother" or "My father." That invites the next question: "Why?"

Journalists learn to answer five questions in every story they write: who, what, why, where, and when? Be prepared to answer all five questions whenever you give an answer. And don't give an answer that doesn't represent the truth. If you don't read books, don't say "I love to read." If you have read some books recently, go over the titles, the authors, and the basic thrust of the books enough times so that you can readily discuss these things when asked about them.

Be sure to carefully review your résumé before going into the interview. Often we write the résumé and never look at it again. Then, while we are sitting across the desk from someone who is in a position to offer us the best job we could ever imagine, an item on the résumé is brought up as a question. Our response? A blank stare; desperate mental scrambling to remember why the item was added to the résumé and what it actually means. You should be prepared to answer any question about any aspect of your background. How do you feel about your parents? Do you have brothers and sisters, and what do they do? Where would you like to be ten years from now? Will you be willing to relocate? The list is endless; the point remains the same. Don't leave anything to chance in an interview. Anticipate the questions, carefully formulate your answers, and deliver them with conviction. That doesn't mean spitting out replies like an automaton. In fact, if you have pat answers ready for certain questions, hesitate a little as you give the answer so that it doesn't appear to be a programmed response. It never hurts to pause a few seconds before starting to give an answer. This creates the impression that you're a thoughtful person. It also gives you an opportunity to make sure you're answering the right question. If you're not certain of what the interviewer means with a question he or she has asked, ask for a clarification.

While you want to exude confidence during the interview, you want to make sure that you don't cross the line into arrogance or aloofness. When you are interviewed for a job, you literally are onstage. That certainly does not mean that you become a character that you're not. What it does mean is that you can't view a job interview as nothing more than some pleasant chitchat in which you get to know each other. In fact, I've been critical of many employers who approach an interview with job candidates in the same manner. For the interviewer, there are a number of rules to follow that will help ensure that the interview will produce the sort of solid, worthwhile information that is necessary when making a decision about whom to hire. People are any company's most important asset, and companies that fail to hire smart suffer the consequences down the road.

Looking for a job is a job. Being interviewed for a job is a performance—not one that presents an inaccurate picture of you, but one in which not only is your best foot forward, but that allows you to indicate to your prospective employer that you're on the ball.

One piece of advice I give those in a position of hiring is: if two people appear to be equally qualified, hire a person who wants the job more. Obviously, if the credentials of candidates are inadequate, their enthusiasm should not be the determining factor. But if you take two or more people who all have similar credentials, experience, and skills, it makes sense to bring into the company the person who is most enthusiastic about the potentials the job offers.

Be enthusiastic. That doesn't mean gushing at every question. A real measure of enthusiasm is how much time and effort you've put into learning about the job being offered, the company, and the industry in which the company functions. Nothing is more flattering to an individual than demonstrated sincere interest in what that person does, who that person is, and how you might benefit that person.

The sweetest sound in the world is our own name. I've seen countless job applicants be unsure of the name of the person interviewing them and, consequently, never use it. If the person interviewing you has a long and difficult name, practice saying it as many times as necessary so that it trips easily off your tongue. Write it out phonetically; that's a good memory jogger.

Do everything you can to personalize the interview.

When I'm to give a speech, I make a special effort to observe what's going on around me between the time I arrive at the location of the speech and actually must go to the podium. I listen for interesting comments made that I can work into my introduction. I make a mental note of significant names in the audience so that I can include them in my talk. Before I travel to a city, I take some time to read about that city, and include in my remarks items of particular interest to that locale. In a word, I try to personalize my speech as much as possible.

You should do the same when going in for a job interview. Did the receptionist or secretary say something interesting about the company? If so, you might find it provides you with an easy opening remark to the person interviewing you. Is the building in which the company is located architecturally unusual? You might mention that. Is there something especially attractive or unusual about the physical surroundings of the office in which you find yourself? Mention that, too.

Are there photographs on the wall that reflect the interviewer's particular interests? Is the furniture especially beautiful or functional? Did you read something about the company in the newspaper that morning?

Again, all of this points to the need to approach a job interview with heightened awareness, attention to detail, and a commitment on your part to present yourself as a candidate for the job who obviously cannot be ignored or dismissed.

The bigger the job, the more important intangible factors seem to be. I've had numerous conversations over the years with top executives about why they chose one candidate over another for high-level positions. One, I remember, was put off by the candidate's poor posture. A limp handshake has been mentioned many times. A leading candidate for a top job lost out because those above him did not want a bald man leading its largest division.

One fellow who was being seriously considered as president and CEO of a solid, middle-size firm later learned that he'd lost out because he wore short black socks to the crucial interview, exposing a hunk of bare leg between sock and cuff.

And I remember an executive's being asked during an interview what he thought of the company's current stock price. He didn't know what the current stock price was, and was not called back again. He should have known. That should be part of everyone's preparation.

I've heard it said many times that bow ties, smoking a pipe, too much jewelry on both men and women, and nervous tics lost people big jobs. This may not seem fair, but it certainly does represent reality.

Hard work pays off in every element of our lives, and a job interview is no exception. In order to leave nothing to chance, we must work hard at preparing ourselves for every eventuality. Yes, there will always be an area for which we have not prepared. When this happens, there is nothing more engaging and impressive than honesty. Admitting "I don't know" is a much better answer than trying to cover up the fact that you don't know something. But then quickly shift the conversation to something you *do* know well. It's important that the interviewer remember you for what you knew, rather than for what you didn't know.

This brings up the question of learning from each interview. No matter how well prepared you are, you will leave certain interviews realizing that there were some aspects of it with which you were not at your best. Did the interviewer bring up questions that you never dreamed would be asked? If so, make a note of them, and include them in your rehearsal for the next interview. Did you feel that one of your answers was inadequate, or represented weakness or a lack of conviction on your part? Be honest with yourself. If there were a couple of minutes with which you were uncomfortable, take the time to analyze why, and restructure your approach to that particular question.

The basic rule for any job interview is to *be prepared*. Those who are generally do well. Those who aren't might not *fail* at the interview, but certainly will not position themselves as front-runners for the job.

No matter what people do with their lives, they will always make some mistakes. Hopefully, our mistakes are few, and our achievements many. What's especially important is to learn from our mistakes and avoid repeating them over and over.

A close friend asked me to spend a little time with her son, who was eminently successful. His earnings were in excess of $150,000, but unfortunately the company he was associated with had been acquired by a much larger one, and his particular function was duplicated by the acquiring company. I gave this young man some advice, which he appreciated, and I'm happy to say it worked. He called me and said, "Bob, I did everything you suggested, had several excellent interviews, and I think I'm going to get an offer on a job I interviewed for yesterday. It's a wonderful company and a sensational opportunity."

I surprised him with this question: "What did you do wrong at the interview?"

He quietly responded, "Absolutely nothing."

I said, "That's impossible. Something always goes wrong."

He repeated, "Nothing went wrong. In fact, we got very friendly, and we went out to lunch together. We talked about many things, and people we know in common. He really seems sincerely interested in me as a person. I even told him my diabetes is under control."

"What did you just say?"

He repeated, "My diabetes is under control."

"Did the interviewer ask you about your diabetes?" I asked.

"No, he didn't even know I had it."

"Didn't you just tell me nothing went wrong? Why would you point out a negative that wasn't asked for? There are millions of diabetics who function normally in this world, and you obviously are one of them. Bringing that up, however, leads me to believe that you probably said a few other things you shouldn't have."

The young man thought for a moment, then said, "You're right. I think I did say a few things that probably weren't smart."

He didn't get that job, but he learned a lesson the hard and expensive way. He managed to find another job and I understand it worked out very well for him.

I often say, "The mouth serves two purposes. One is to present your thoughts effectively. The other is to provide a place in which to put your foot. Your choice!"

The world in which you seek a better job is certainly

not the same as it was before. But the rules of interchange between two individuals really haven't changed. The interviewer has to fill a job, and wants the choice he or she makes to be a wise one. You, seeking the job, must convince that person that not hiring you would be a dreadful mistake. Nothing new there.

Now, here are a couple of hints you may find helpful.

We found through research that the last person interviewed was hired 55.8 percent of the time, while the first person interviewed got the job in only 17.6 percent of the cases. It appears that many employers are heeding the old baseball adage about never hitting the first ball pitched. It doesn't work in baseball, and it certainly doesn't work in hiring. But, be that as it may, it's a fact of life. If you suspect you're going to be the first person interviewed, try to do something about shifting the date. However, be cautious; don't say anything that will jeopardize getting the interview or antagonize the interviewer. If the interviewer asks you whether, as an example, Tuesday, Wednesday, or Thursday would be okay, take Thursday.

We did an additional survey through Burke Marketing Research that indicated that Monday is, by far, the worst day of the week to be interviewed for a job. The worst time for a job interview is late afternoon.

This information may prove to be useful, but I caution you to handle it with care—don't lose the interview by manipulating dates and time. You could say, "I'd be happy to meet with you at four-thirty, but I'd prefer eleven, if you don't mind."

Reminders on Being Interviewed

≡ A job interview isn't just a pleasant chat. Be prepared.

≡ Rehearse. Know the selling points you intend to bring up no matter what questions are asked.

≡ Anticipate as many questions as possible.

≡ Learn from every interview. Always ask yourself, "What did I do wrong, and what worked particularly well?"

≡ Always assume that when you answer one question, there will be a follow-up, usually in search of specifics.

≡ Carefully review your résumé before going into an interview.

≡ Don't confuse confidence with arrogance.

≡ Be enthusiastic. Be the candidate who is perceived as wanting the job the most.

≡ Research the company and the background of your interviewer, if possible.

≡ Be nice to everyone.

22 · ASK FOR THE JOB

You gotta ask!

EVERY GOOD SALESPERSON KNOWS THAT ONE OF the keys to success is to ask for the order. We've all dealt with salesmen and saleswomen who are engaging, know the product they're selling, present it with enthusiasm and point out why we can't live without it, are likable, gain our confidence, and do everything right...except they don't ask us to buy. So we don't.

The same situation holds true for the job seeker. The credentials you bring to a position might be perfect for it. You make a good appearance, answer all the questions smoothly and with substance, yet don't get the job because, like the salesperson above, you haven't asked for it.

There are many ways of asking for a job without sounding overly aggressive. Actually, asking for a job you want is a continuous process. The thank-you letter you send after the first interview should also include a statement of your continuing interest in the job for which you're being considered—a line like "I have even more interest in the job now that we've had a chance to meet and talk about it" or "I would like very much to further pursue the possibility of my working for you and the company, and look forward to a chance to discuss that in the near future."

If, after your final interview, you are convinced that you want to work for the company, say so. I remember years ago when a man came to our offices as an applicant for a controller's job with our organization. I decided that he wasn't right for it, and suggested that we might find him a good position with another company. He looked me straight in the eye and said, "Mr. Half, I want to work for *you*, and will consider any position you might be able to offer me."

No one had ever said that to me before, and no one has since. The end result was that we did find a spot for this person, and he turned out to be a loyal and productive employee for many years.

Because employers and interviewers are nothing more than human beings, they deal from the same base of insecurities that you, the job seeker, does. Some are reluctant to offer a job because they don't want to be turned down. Some employers operate on the assumption that a candidate must make it plain that he or she wants the job before it will be offered. If you don't say that you want the job, you'll never have an offer from this type of employer.

Avoid high pressure. You can gracefully ask for the job by saying, "I know you have a number of good candidates to consider, Mr. Smith, but I do want you to know that I would like very much to work for you here at the XYZ Company. I know I'll be able to contribute something positive, and I assure you if you do hire me, I won't let you down."

I guarantee you one thing: if you take this approach with a job you really want, you'll stand out, because unless all the candidates you're competing with have also read and followed this book, few will be that direct in asking for the job.

Asking for what you want shouldn't be confined to

getting a job, however. People fail to achieve many things, personally and professionally, throughout their lives because they don't make it clear what they want. People mumble an order to a counterperson in a deli and then complain that they got mustard instead of mayonnaise. When people in a relationship fail to let each other know what it is they need and want, they seldom get it, and very often the relationship suffers for it.

In business, a boss can't be expected to be a mind reader. If you feel you deserve a raise or a promotion, and you have the tangible evidence of performance to back you up, you must ask for it. The worst that can happen is that your request is denied, but it will stay in your boss's mind and perhaps trigger a future raise quicker than otherwise. If a new position opens up within the company that you would like to be considered for, you must make your desire known to those who can put it into effect.

In line with asking for what you want is being sure that you communicate your needs and wishes properly. Again, that need to sharpen our communication skills comes into play. Most people make their wishes known in an indirect, circumspect manner and then don't understand why their request isn't acted upon. How many letters do we receive in a lifetime that are filled with vague, unnecessary phrases and go on at length, the actual reason for writing the letter buried somewhere in all the verbiage? An effective letter begins with a simple statement of why the letter has been written in the first place. Then it goes on to provide material to substantiate the request.

The same holds true in speech. It is so frustrating to sit with someone who wants something that could be stated in six or eight words, yet spends minutes getting to the point.

That doesn't mean you have to be blunt or rude. But be direct and let the other person know precisely what it is you want. If it's a job, say you want it. Your chances of getting it will be enhanced.

The exact language you use in asking for the job will vary from person to person. Obviously, a direct statement like "I really want this job" will be handled nicely by certain people. For others, it might smack of indicating undue need, even desperation. Here are some other ways to ask for the job that not only accomplish that goal but indicate to the employer your level of enthusiasm and confidence:

"I just want to say that if you hire me, I won't let you down."

"You'll always be able to count on me."

"I'll always give you more than you expect."

"Hire me and I can assure you I'll do an excellent job."

"I'm anxious to prove to you that I can handle this job...and more."

"I want this job, and I assure you you won't be sorry if you hire me."

"This job fits my background and abilities to a *t*."

23·INVESTIGATE THE COMPANY

Tell me something about this company

ONE OF THE MOST SIGNIFICANT CHANGES OVER the past forty years is in the attitude of young people coming into the work force. Decades ago the notion that work should be fulfilling, and even fun, was considered ridiculous. Work represented toil and sweat, and workers viewed it as exactly that. The primary incentive was pay, hopefully enough to raise a family and live a decent life outside the company.

Today, every survey—including some I've commissioned—indicates that money is no longer the primary motivation for American workers. Today's breed of success seeker wants challenge and autonomy, psychic recognition, and freedom to explore new ideas. Unfortunately, too large a percentage of American management hasn't recognized this, and as a result fails to attract or keep the best and the brightest.

A paradox of this situation is that although millions of jobs are being lost, it is still a "buyers' market" for young men and women with considerable knowledge and skills to offer. These rising stars know that they are needed, and can afford to be choosy when it comes to accepting a job. Not *too* choosy, however. As I said in chapter 4, seeking a "dream job" is almost invariably a futile exercise. But, within the limits of reason, don't sell yourself short. That's why it's important to save money while you are employed. If you don't know how to pay the rent next month, you lose your options when it comes to employment, and find yourself making decisions out of desperation, rather than being able to turn down a job that lacks many of the things that are important to you.

If you are one of these rising stars, you owe it to yourself and, by extension, to a company to be secure in your mind that if a job is offered to you, it's going to make you happy and fulfilled. It's often hard to ascertain this until you've actually been on the job for a while, but you should do everything in your power to make that determination before accepting an offer.

Ask questions. Workers years ago felt this was inappropriate, and job interviews were very much a one-way street. The company asked questions about you and made a determination whether you were worthy of being employed there. Today, it is perfectly acceptable, even smart, to interview the company at the same time the company is interviewing you.

To some, asking questions of a potential employer means going through a boilerplate list of inquiries about the number of vacation days, medical benefits, pension plans, and other nitty-gritty. Those kinds of questions should be asked, of course, but later—as an adjunct. Save those questions for when you're close to being offered the job, and make them part of your salary negotiations.

Your basic line of questioning should focus upon the management philosophy under which you'll be working: the opportunities for being independent within the framework of a department's and company's goals, the reporting structure in which you'll be positioned, learning opportunities within the company, both formal and informal, and a reasonable understanding of opportunities for advancement for someone who not only does his or her job but goes beyond that.

A standard question asked of job candidates is "Where do you see yourself ten years from now?" I don't like answering a question with another question, because that usually leaves both questions unanswered, but sometimes it's reasonable for you to ask, "Where do you think I *can* be in this company, provided I do the sort of job I know I'm capable of doing?"

You will, of course, have to trust the answers given you by the person doing the interviewing. That's understandable, because, after all, the interviewer hopefully will trust the answers you've given to questions, and may very well verify them by reference checking. But because an interview should be a two-way street, you can apply the same intuition in judging the person with whom you're interviewing as that person is doing with you. One word of caution, however: don't judge an entire company by one or two individuals. We've all had experiences with a rude or inept individual and ended up judging an entire company based upon one person's behavior. A rude bank teller at one branch can cause us to think poorly of the bank as an entity. A surly flight attendant causes us to brand the airline "no good." We know, of course, that this is irrational, that we shouldn't make such broad judgments based on a narrow experience, but often we do, unless we remind ourselves of the folly it represents.

The person interviewing you may be an unpleasant human being, or even downright nasty. It behooves you to look beyond that; your contact with others in the company will give you a more balanced picture. Of course, if the person interviewing you will be your immediate supervisor, that lends a lot more weight to the decision you'll have to make, but even then, if the company is growing and offers excellent opportunities, the chances may be very good that you'll be able to advance beyond that supervisor and establish a wonderful career for yourself.

If the company in which you're interested is in an industry that you've been working in right along, it becomes much easier to gain insight into how the company functions and whether employees there are satisfied. Use your network again, this time to find out more about the internal workings of the company. Of course, you must always filter comments and weigh the worth of them based upon your assessment of the individual giving them. Someone who was fired from a company is obviously not going to have many good things to say about it. On the other hand, someone who is disgruntled in his or her present employment with another company is likely to view the one you're seeking a position with as better than it is.

Because our world has become intensely competitive, there are corporations that oversell the advantages of working for them as they compete to hire the best and brightest available people. It's difficult to determine whether the job offered you will prove to be as good as it was painted by those with whom you came into contact. Again, it pays to take whatever steps are necessary to get a handle on this before accepting a job. See if you can talk to the person you would be replacing, or others in the department in which you would be working. By all means ask for a tour of the facilities, especially the area in which you would be spending your days. We've come a long way since the sweatshops that brought about unionism, but it's amazing how many companies today do not understand the need to provide a pleasant, safe, and healthy work environment. I'm certainly not suggesting turning down a job because the office faces south while you would prefer windows that face west, or even because the office you'll be in doesn't have windows at all. But recognize that you will be spending the largest portion of your waking hours in that place and at that job.

If you can take a tour, be astute enough to recognize whether the people working there seem productive and happy, or whether a pervasive veil of gloom hangs over things. If management respects—and, equally important, trusts—them, there will be a spark evident in almost everyone.

If you decide to take a job after having done your homework, and after having taken every opportunity to learn about the company, go into it with unabashed enthusiasm and the determination to succeed. However, if you have been sold a bill of goods and you find yourself in an unpleasant and stagnant environment, get out fast. Again, having some savings to back you up makes that decision a lot easier, but even if you don't, recognize that to hang in may only do you harm over the long haul.

I have a friend who'd worked alone for many years. He decided he needed the stimulation of working with other people, and applied for an excellent job with a company for which he used to work, which he had left on the best of terms. He was hired, and started work on a Monday. On Friday of that week, he went to his boss and said he'd made a mistake and intended to leave. My friend told me that this was the most difficult decision he had ever had to make, and one of the most awkward situations he'd ever been in. But he knew instinctively that his reasons for taking the job were wrong (he was running away from something, not seeking something better), and had to do it. It caused a great deal of rancor, especially with his immediate boss, who had just sent out a press release to all the trade magazines in that industry announcing my friend's appointment to this important position. But he stuck with his decision and was gone six weeks later, after a replacement had been found.

That might be extreme, and his circumstances certainly do not reflect those of most employees, but the message is clear. However, be realistic in evaluating your situation. While jobs today perhaps should be exciting and fulfilling, and even offer a sense of fun and challenge, every job carries with it certain tedium, some unpleasant people, and a host of other factors that may not suit you perfectly. Make sure the situation is intolerable before making a drastic decision to leave a job after only a short time.

24 · ANSWER ADS A SECOND TIME

What do I have to lose?

YOU SPOTTED AN AD IN THE NEWSPAPER FOR A job that seems perfect for you. Every aspect of your background applies, and you have extensive experience in the industry indicated in the ad. You sent off a customized résumé that was perfect in every detail. Your covering letter was to the point and well written. Then you waited. Nothing.

Two weeks later, you see the same ad in the paper. How could they have passed me up, you wonder? Should I take another stab at it?

Most people don't make another attempt in such a situation. They're content to wallow in their aggravation and frustration. That's a mistake. It could be that your initial response got lost in the mailroom, or in a tall pile of responses that sit on the hiring executive's desk.

The question you have to ask yourself when this occurs—and it does occur with regularity—is what you have to lose by responding to the same ad again. A postage stamp, a piece of stationery, and a bit of your time? Those are small expenditures compared to the potential gain. I urge you to try again. If you come up with the right kind of letter for this second attempt, you could land that better job you've been yearning for. I agree that the odds are against you, but even hundred-to-one-shot racehorses win once in a hundred times.

What I suggest is to be aggressive in your second letter. It might start something like this:

"You might have seen my résumé a few weeks ago, but then again, you might not have ..."

As I mentioned earlier, your chances of succeeding with this approach are not great. But nothing ventured, nothing gained. I recommend that you include second attempts in your bag of job-seeking techniques.

Remember, you have everything to gain, and nothing to lose.

25· HOW LONG TO FIND A BETTER JOB?

It takes more time when time is no problem

PEOPLE GIVING ADVICE OF ANY KIND THAT IS BASI-cally intangible seem to enjoy creating formulas to give their advice a feeling of substance. That's as true in the employment field as in any other.

Over the years, employment counselors—especially those who've written books on the subject—have tried to come up with formulas to indicate how long you should expect to be out of work or, if employed, how long it will take you to find a better job. Some of the formulas are wonderfully inventive. Some are based upon a few good ideas, and incorporate a number of tangible factors such as salary, years of experience, market conditions, personal commitment, and the like. And there have been others that are downright silly, in my estimation.

Before I go any further and am accused of being hypocritical by those readers of this book who also read my previous book on getting jobs (*The Robert Half Way to Get Hired in Today's Job Market*, published in 1981 by Rawson/Wade), I admit that I attempted in that earlier work to come up with just such a formula on how long it might take to get a job. My reaction in retrospect is that it was a good formula but, like all others, doesn't have much validity in this present world (whether it had validity years ago will have to remain conjecture, and be judged by those job seekers who used it).

The fact is that looking for a better job, whether as an employed person or unemployed, involves so many intangible and subjective elements that no formula can be safely applied to any individual. Still, I felt it necessary to touch upon the question of how long it takes to get a job in order to help the readers of this book recognize that many variables are involved and that one should not give up too quickly. Most important, I truly feel that if you do what this book recommends, you'll take considerably less time than were you to go after a better job without incorporating its advice into your overall plan.

Most formulas that have been concocted deal with the number of months it will take to find employment. Suppose these formulas result in an estimate that a certain salaried job would take, on the average, six months to find. But, also suppose that one person in that salary range puts in fifty hours a week looking for a job and another person puts in only ten hours a week. Obviously, the person putting in more time and effort is likely to find a better job faster than the one putting in less time and effort.

Here, too, however, there are myriad factors that might render that judgment inaccurate. An inept job seeker devoting fifty hours a week might take a lot longer than an especially sharp, knowledgeable, and experienced person putting in only a few hours a week. Add the vagaries of geography, ability to see oneself in an interview, the right résumé, the size and quality of the network, and a host of other factors and you can see why formulas simply don't work.

Let's look at the factors that will really determine how long it takes you to find your better job.

If you're employed in a good job, with a good company in a solid industry, and have virtually no chance of losing your job in the near future, looking for a better one will undoubtedly take a long time. The reason is simple: you're only passively looking for a job, and will find one only if it's "perfect" and handed to you on a silver platter. Many people keep their eyes open for an opportunity that would simply be too good to pass up.

Take another person who stands little chance of losing a job, but is working for a company that is running into problems, or is a takeover candidate, or is in an industry that is declining, and chances are there will be more interest in exploring new opportunities, which, by extension, will produce a better job faster.

Are you a generalist or a specialist? Your answer to this will help determine how long it takes for you to land a better job or, if between jobs, any job at all. It almost always takes longer for a specialist to find and land a new job, the level of difficulty in direct proportion to the degree of specialization. The number of openings for specialists in any field is naturally fewer than openings for generalists. Of course, specialists are usually highly paid in return for their special knowledge, but the specialist also runs the risk of falling behind as changes occur in the specialty. A data processor steeped in a certain combination of hardware and software might suddenly find that his or her expertise is approaching obsolescence. Unless that person has been keeping up-to-date all along (which is hard to do), those companies that have instituted the new system may not be available to that job seeker.

Generalists, on the other hand, while having more job opportunities available to them, are usually not paid as much as specialists. They also sometimes become so generalized in their skills and knowledge (the jack-of-all-trades, master-of-none person) that it's virtually impossible to categorize them when looking to fill a job. I've asked so many generalists, "What do you do? What is it you want?" The answer is invariably "I can do anything." Not very helpful to a personnel manager or recruiter.

Then again, generalists are the people who generally end up heading companies and corporations because of their broad knowledge of the many workings of that business.

How good—or bad—are your references? If you don't have good references, your job search will probably take longer, unless you run across a situation in which the hiring company doesn't care about your bad references, or doesn't bother to check them at all. If you're one of those people who've burned a series of bridges when leaving jobs, you've painted yourself into a corner from which it is difficult to extricate yourself.

How competitive are you? You should take the time to rate yourself in terms of competitiveness. An honest evaluation of your education, experience, knowledge, appearance, and skill at finding new and better jobs will help determine how long it will take you to succeed. If you rate high on the competitive scale, chances are you'll be hired faster than someone who rates lower.

While you're analyzing your competitiveness, also take stock of your personal characteristics. Do you tend to be sloppy in your dress and grooming? Are you a pleasant person, or does a sour face reflect a basically grouchy personality? Are you positive and enthusiastic, or do you tend to see the glass as perpetually being half empty? Companies that market a product spend huge amounts of time and money analyzing what their product looks like, whether it is appealing to the eye, and whether it sends off silent signals of being quality, a product that will enhance a consumer's life. When looking for a job, *you* are the product, and you should pay significant attention to what your product looks like, as well as the signals it gives off.

Are you a person who is making too many demands and imposing too many conditions on the type of employment you'll accept? Have you set unrealistic restrictions on how much time you're willing to travel, or have you narrowed down the places to which you are willing to relocate to a restrictive few? Many companies, particularly larger ones, expect their employees to be willing to relocate if the need arises, and to take whatever travel is necessary to get the job done. The more you've narrowed your willingness in these areas, the longer it will take you to get a job. Again, this might not be true if other factors override these considerations, but, in general, the more restrictions you put on jobs you'll accept, the longer your job search will take.

For many people, arbitrary salary demands rule out finding a better job. Are you realistic in the kind of money you think you're worth and in evaluating the salaries that are generally paid in your industry or profession for people with your qualifications? If you're capable only of jobs that pay the minimum wage, you may be hired tomorrow. If you're making $40,000 and won't move for anything less than $150,000, you're not realistic and are in for a long wait. Of course, if you are employed you can afford to sit it out and wait for a job with a high salary to come your way. If you're unemployed and you are being unrealistic in what you will accept, you are going to overlook many splendid opportunities to get back into the workplace and once again build a solid base from which to advance your career. What I'm saying is be flexible, depending upon circumstances.

Have you learned how to toot your own horn in a palatable way? Because you are a "product," you must sell yourself. If you are not good at this, chances are you will take longer to find a better job than someone who is comfortable with the art and skill of selling him- or herself to a new employer. In line with this, are you willing to *ask* (not plead) for a job, not only verbally but in your attitude and in the way you present yourself?

Finally, a major determining factor in how quickly you find a better job is how much time, effort, and dedication you are willing to put into it. Are you committed to an intensive job search, or are you approaching it passively, waiting for a stroke of luck to come from the heavens, or for someone to immediately think of you when an opening occurs, even though you haven't kept in regular touch?

I think you can see why a formula for how long it will take to find a better job is just an academic exercise.

On the other side of the coin, it is possible to evaluate, in general, how long any given *company* might take to make a hiring decision. Robert Half International commissioned an independent research survey in which vice-presidents and personnel directors were asked how long, on the average, it took for their companies to fill a position. We also asked how many people in the company, on the average, will interview a candidate once the company has decided to go to that step. The results were interesting.

They reported that it takes an average of three and a half months to fill a top-management position, two months to fill a middle-management position, and one and a half months to fill a staff position.

In answer to the question about how many people will interview a job candidate, the respondents to the survey indicated that an average of five will interview a candidate for a top-management position, four for someone who is being considered for a middle-management position, and three people for a man or woman being considered for a staff position.

In my experience, medium and small companies usually conduct fewer interviews and take less time to fill positions. The important point here is that it generally takes a job seeker longer to find a job than a company to hire someone. The reason for this is obvious: the job seeker must first locate a number of job opportunities; go through the process of applying for them; endure the interview process; attract a job offer; and then decide if it's suitable.

No matter how untenable it is to attempt to formularize the length of time it will take you to find a job, there will always be people who will try to use formulas and, in many cases, regret the fact that they did. I've seen this happen with people who decide to seek a better job and quit their current employment before starting that search. They've figured it all out with one formula or another and determined, let's say, that they will find their new and better job within 1.75 months. When the fourth month of unemployment rolls around, they begin to rethink the wisdom of their actions.

How quickly you find another job will be determined almost exclusively by you, not by outside factors.

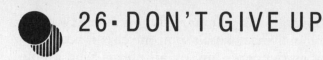

26 · DON'T GIVE UP

Sorry, we've hired someone else

IF YOU DON'T GET THE JOB YOU REALLY WANT, don't write it off.

Sometimes a company hires a new person and one of two things happens:

1. The newly hired person changes his or her mind at the last minute and accepts a job with another firm, usually a hoped-for but delayed job offer.

2. Or the new person begins work and quickly leaves, either because the job doesn't match up to expectations or because the supervisor realizes a terrible mistake has been made and fires the new hire.

In either case, the company now has a problem. Smart employers, faced with this dilemma, will immediately contact others who'd been favorably considered for the job to see if they're still available. Most managers won't do this, however, if only out of embarrassment.

That's why I urge job seekers to call the company that has turned them down and indicate a continuing interest in working for that company. I also think it is as appropriate to send a note following being turned down

181

as it is sending a thank-you note after an interview. Even though a company has chosen someone else, if you know you made a good impression, by all means send a note mildly expressing your disappointment in the decision and indicating your continued strong interest in working for that company. Yes, this necessitates admitting to the company that turned you down that you are still looking, but so what? I've seen this approach work, and everyone benefits from it—the company gets a good person, and a good person gets a good job.

27 · MAKE SURE THE JOB OFFER IS FIRM

I just got a great job...I think

HAVE YOU EVER MET PEOPLE WHO ONLY HEAR what they want to hear, no matter what is said?

Everyone who has spent any time in the personnel services industry has met lots of them. Generally they're dreamers, and we all know dreamers never let the facts get in the way of a good dream.

Here's what happens with these people. They go through the interview process in search of a job and things are going well. In fact, the interviewer, who will be their direct supervisor, says something like, "I really would like to have you in this job. So far, of everyone I've seen, you impress me the most."

Every job seeker would love to hear that. The difference is that most job seekers will take it for exactly what it is: a positive comment about their chances *without* a job offer's having been made.

The dreamer doesn't see it that way. The dreamer floats out of the office, announces to friends and family that the job has been offered or says something like "It's in the bag," and then proceeds to quit his or her current job or, if out of work, stops looking any further.

Then comes the call: "Sorry, but we've decided on someone else."

That represents big trouble for the dreamer.

The dreamer may have received a legitimate job offer, but with the provision that his or her references prove satisfactory. Perhaps a physical is involved before the final offer can be made, or other administrative details must be worked out to the employer's satisfaction.

Again, those potential stumbling blocks are ignored, and the dreamer plays out the same scenario of announcing a new job and quitting the existing one, or holding back on pursuing other leads. Then a reference doesn't check out, or someone else in the company has a reason for not hiring this individual, or a decision is made to not fill the opening at all.

Sometimes a dreamer projects rather than dealing with the reality of the moment. In this case, the interviewer indicates that there is the *potential* of advancing to a vice-presidency one day. The dreamer knows vice-presidents in that company are never paid less than $100,000 a year. So the dreamer takes the job and thinks only of the VP title and the $100,000. The dreamer tells her husband, "They said I'd be vice-president in six months." Of course, that was never said, but the dreamer is carried away with wishful thinking. Six months go by and the dreamer is angry. "They lied to me," she tells her husband, when, in fact, no one lied to anyone.

My advice has always been that until a firm job offer has been made and a starting date has been established, keep your mouth shut, continue to look for a new job with the same enthusiasm and energy as before, and, if you're employed, keep working very hard at your present job.

Finally, on this subject, listen carefully to what a prospective employer says, and don't embellish it with your own wishful thinking.

28 · NEGOTIATING SALARY

That's all? I can't afford to work for that

ONE OF THE BIGGEST MISTAKES PEOPLE MAKE IN seeking a better job is to bring up the question of salary too early in the process.

Obviously, any job seeker has a general sense of what a job will pay prior to applying for it. If you've learned of an opening through a newspaper ad, the salary or salary range will generally be part of the ad. A recruiter will certainly know the salary range and will inform you of it before sending you for an interview. Also, you should be able to learn through your network what jobs of this type generally pay throughout the industry. In other words, you go after a job having a pretty good idea of the most you can expect to be paid at the start. The minimum will certainly be determined by you, and will be a combination of what you realistically feel your skills and knowledge are worth and what bottom-line figure you need to live on. Don't automatically rule out jobs, however, that may pay less than your predetermined minimum but offer you the sort of challenge and future opportunities that you've been seeking. This comment may even apply if you're presently employed. Look at it this way. The chances are you've already invested a lot of time finding this job lead, and may have had preliminary interviews. But if you're highly qualified, you may be missing a jackpot. I know some instances where the right person got double what the firm originally intended to pay.

The reason you should try to put off any discussion of salary as long as possible is that if you wait until the company has decided that *you* are the person it wants, you are in a stronger bargaining position. The company is more likely to go to its upper limits of the salary range for that particular job once they've picked you, rather than have to continue looking.

If you're asked early in the interviewing process how much money you're seeking, one way to postpone it is to answer "I really would prefer to make that determination after I've had a chance to explore the potentials of working here and the opportunity for advancement." That generally will do it. Don't, however, say you're more interested in the potentials for advancement *only* as a way to postpone the discussion of salary. Mean it! A job with a good future may mean more than one in which you earn an additional thousand dollars or so but do not get the opportunity to advance into positions of greater responsibility, and substantially more pay, a few years down the road. Try to look to the future as much as possible when making decisions like this, based upon your realistic needs in order to live a decent life.

Naturally, if pressed, you may have to come up with a figure, hopefully one that you have given careful consideration to before arriving for the interview. That should be part of your rehearsal—but be realistic, both up and down. Don't ask for a salary that is out of line with what others in similar positions are earning, or is unreasonable considering how much experience and background you bring to the job. On the other hand, don't underestimate yourself. People with low self-esteem seem to go through their entire working lives being paid less than what their counterparts are earning for doing similar work.

Sometimes you can put off committing yourself to a salary requirement by saying: "The starting salary is not my most important consideration. As you know, I'm earning $45,000 a year now. If you don't mind, let's postpone this discussion until you have a better idea of what I can do for you and I have a chance to know a little more about the job and the company."

When considering whether your current salary or one that's been offered you is sufficient, keep inflation in mind. The *Kiplinger Washington Letter* analyzed what a 1988 salary would be worth in ten years, taking into account various rates of inflation. An important point was made that even though estimates on inflation over the next decade are low (anywhere from 4 to 6 percent), the erosion of buying power represented by those "low" figures is startling.

Someone making $20,000 in 1990 would need to be making $33,000 just to break even ten years from now at an inflation rate of 5 percent. That same person earning $20,000 in 1990 would need to earn $36,000 if the inflation rate were 6 percent.

An individual making $70,000 in 1990 would need a salary of $114,000 at a 5 percent inflation rate, and $125,000 at a 6 percent rate of inflation.

The point for job seekers is that if you started the job you're presently in at a salary of, let's say, $30,000, stay in the job for the next ten years, and receive regular increases that, at the end of ten years, bring you up to $45,000, you've lost, in effect, $9,000 if the inflation rate over those ten years is 6 percent.

It's vitally important to view job changes on a long-term basis. If you're unemployed, you don't have this luxury unless you've stashed away enough money to live on while you are being selective in what job to take. Don't be lulled by claims that the inflation rate will *only* be 6 percent over the next decade. Six percent makes a big difference in what your hard-earned dollars will buy.

Sometimes offering to work for *nothing* makes sense. Let's say you've found exactly the job you want. It comes as close to being your ideal job as possible. But the salary you're asking threatens to eliminate you from consideration. Or they're reluctant to hire you because you do not have enough of the required years of experience. If you can manage it personally, suggest that you be hired for a specified period of time—maybe a month—without pay, with the understanding that if you prove how valuable you know you can be in that job, you'll be hired permanently and receive the salary you've asked for. This is a good attention-getter. The company cannot legally hire you without paying the minimum salary, and you should qualify "working free" with the comment "Of course, you'll have to pay a token to me for legal reasons—the minimum wage during this brief trial period."

I don't recommend this approach in general, but some good men and women have found success by taking this road. Two factors must be in place—that you're unemployed and that the opportunity the job provides is excellent.

Obviously, for many occupations it would be impossible for an employer to be positive that you're the right person for the job. But the trial period gives a boss a lot more information than without it. Your ability to get along, your willingness to work hard, and your facility for catching on and following instructions are all traits that an employer will observe, and use when deciding whether to take you on as a permanent employee.

29·EMPLOYMENT CONTRACTS

Put it in black and white

IN THE PAST, THE MAJOR REASON COMPANIES DID not like to enter into employment agreements was that they were basically for the protection of the employee. Few benefits accrued to the company except to prevent the employee from leaving to join a competitor.

But, here again, times have changed in this world, and employers have discovered an important reason they may want to write an employment agreement—being able to fire at will.

It used to be the inalienable right of an employer to fire an employee for any reason whatsoever, at any time, and with no severance pay if so desired. Things are different now. Employees have sued and won judgments in the courts based upon the implication that the employer must have valid reasons to discharge an employee, and, of course, the validity of those reasons must be determined by a jury. The employment agreement may be one of several ways the employer can defend against such lawsuits if the contract makes it clear that the employer has the right to fire at will, provided there's a caveat explaining what constitutes cause for discharge.

Even though there is this new advantage to a company in writing employment agreements, they generally reserve them for high-level positions within the corporation. For a lower-level employee seeking a job, it is not only probably futile to ask for a written contract, it could dash your chances of being hired at all.

Still, because the benefits are great to some employees, the questions of a written contract might not be a bad idea to raise if you think the atmosphere is conducive to risks, and particularly if taking the job means you have to relocate out of town.

Bear in mind that employment contracts to you are mainly nothing more than "exit contracts." In other words, the terms of your leaving a job are spelled out and ensure you a certain amount of severance pay, continuing use of the company's services and facilities—things like that.

Unless you can offer to a company skills considerably above and beyond those of others seeking the same position, and you're giving up a good job to join the new company, your chances of being given a written employment agreement, even today, are slender at best unless you qualify for a top-management job.

There is another type of employment agreement, in letter form, and that simply spells out what has been promised you should you take the job. If there are stock options, guaranteed bonuses based upon your performance level and the company's, and other additional compensation, any company offering these things should be willing to put them in writing. It is not uncommon to put into this type of agreement a severance clause, which requires the employer to pay the employee a stipulated amount of severance pay in the event of termination without cause.

But if that isn't the accepted practice at the company with which you're seeking employment, it's unlikely for them to make an exception for you. Demanding that kind of agreement before accepting a job is akin to a man or woman demanding a prenuptial agreement before marrying. There certainly are good reasons for premarital agreements, especially in second marriages where there are children from previous marriages to be protected. Still, a prenuptial agreement, no matter how well-meaning, sets up an atmosphere of distrust that can get in the way of a smooth and happy beginning to the new union.

The same atmosphere of distrust is created in business when an employee *insists* upon having everything in writing.

My suggestion is that unless you truly don't need the job you've been offered, and are unwilling to make a change unless you have everything in writing—ask for it. If it backfires on you, accept that graciously and continue your job search until you find a company that is willing to meet this demand. If you're unemployed and are not required to move out of town, my advice is not to ask for any form of contract.

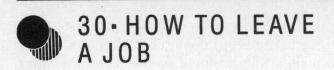

30·HOW TO LEAVE A JOB

The "how not to burn your bridges" chapter

THERE ARE TWO MAIN REASONS FOR LEAVING A job: either you've found a better one or you've been dismissed by your current employer. In either case, the manner in which you depart can play an important role in how you do in the future.

Successfully leaving a job demands as much thought and adherence to certain principles as looking for a new one. Every step you take should be directed at leaving on a positive note, no matter how unpleasant the circumstances leading up to your departure might have been. The old "small world" adage is certainly true in business, particularly within similar industries. The examples of former bosses once again entering a person's professional life are legion. In fact, I've known of hundreds of men and women who were invited back—sometimes years later— for bigger and better jobs in the firm they left.

Let's focus on how to leave a job from which you've resigned because you've found a better one.

Bear in mind that if you've developed a close and pleasant working relationship with your current boss, your decision to accept a job elsewhere might be taken as a sign of personal rejection, especially if your boss perceives him- or herself as having been good to you. You might not feel as though you've been treated as magnanimously as your boss does, but that doesn't matter. If wounded feelings are there, do what you can to salve them.

Keep everything on a professional plane. No matter what negative feelings exist in you, no matter what your reasons for resigning, shelve them in the interest of departing on a compatible note. During discussions with your boss about why you're leaving, stick to the idea that your decision is based upon career objectives. Point out the advantages the new job will provide you, without indicating that you were dissatisfied with your present one. Do not inject personal and negative comments about your boss, your job, or the company itself.

In many firms today, you'll be asked to speak with people other than your immediate supervisor. The concept of the "exit interview" is a popular one, and makes sense from a company's point of view. It wants to know what has caused a good employee to leave. This can help a company determine areas in which it might be deficient, especially where personnel are concerned. It's also good public relations for the company. Rather than have you leave with negative thoughts and feelings, which, naturally, will be expressed to others in your industry, the exit interview can help smooth these things out.

The same rules apply during an exit interview as when talking with your boss. Keep everything positive and professional. You've made a decision to leave because of what you consider to be a better career opportunity for yourself. Perhaps there is more money, a better title, increased responsibility. Those are the reasons to give for leaving a job. To spout personal complaints only sours your present employer on you.

When we're young, we often don't look very far into

the future. Believe me, the company you're leaving and its people will perhaps once again play a role in your search for career success. Keep each bridge intact; burned bridges can seldom be crossed again.

Assuming your exit interview is not with your boss, questions might be asked about your views of how the company, or your specific department, is being run. I don't believe you should offer such comments. If you have some positive and constructive ideas about how to improve things in your department, share those ideas only with your boss.

Anything negative you say to an exit interviewer other than your boss might be conceived as negative comments about the person who supervised the activities of your department. Leaving a job is a time to practice restraint. It often isn't easy, but the potential rewards make it worthwhile.

When you've been offered a new and better job, and have decided to accept it, you should resign from your present employer in two ways.

First, tell your boss that you've decided to take a new position and will be leaving. Then write a brief formal letter of resignation addressed to your boss, with a copy to the head of personnel or human resources—they'll keep it on file. The reason a letter is so important is that a few years from now, your boss may be gone, and so might the personnel executive who was there when you left. That means that if a new employer is checking references and there is no written record of the fact that you resigned and departed in a positive light, the new personnel director at your former employer might not be aware of those facts.

Like your verbal comments to your boss, colleagues, and exit interviewer, the letter should be positive. It needn't be long; in fact, it shouldn't be. Simply state that after, let's say, eight years with your present company, you have elected to leave to take a new position. (Spell out what that new position is and what company it is with.) Indicate that your years with your present company have been fruitful and rewarding. You might say how much you've learned, and could comment that you're proud of what you'd been able to accomplish. Also indicate that the decision you've made was difficult because of how much you've enjoyed your years with the company. Remember, this is a letter for the record. Curb any inclination to slip in a subtle criticism of the company or of an individual. Positive and straightforward— that's the approach to take with a resignation letter.

Your new employer will ask when you can start. If you're unemployed, "tomorrow" is as good an answer as any. But if you're leaving a job for a better one, give as much notice as possible. Even if the new employer puts pressure on you, hold fast to your commitment to give your current employer a fair amount of time to adjust to your departure. In almost every case, new employers will respect that commitment because they know you'll give them the same courtesy should you decide to leave them in the future. It's the same principle as not revealing secrets of your current employer. If you'll do it to *them*, there's no reason to think you won't do it to someone else.

If the pressure is really on you to start a new job sooner than a month, do what the woman in chapter 7 did when faced with that situation: offer to spend a portion of your spare time getting involved in your new job even though you haven't officially come on board as an employee.

If you can manage it, tack on an extra week so that you have some time between jobs to regroup and organize yourself. I certainly wouldn't hold out for that if it represents an unreasonable demand to a new boss, but most people understand our need for a break between jobs, no matter how brief. However, also bear in mind that the longer you take to report to your new job, the more time the employer has to change its mind, for whatever reason.

Leaving sometimes creates an awkward situation with fellow employees. Leaving for a better job is naturally a time of exuberance and celebration. You've gone after that better spot and have landed it, and there is a natural tendency to crow about it to those with whom you've shared your working life. Yes, demonstrate your enthusiasm for the move, but don't go overboard. While most of your colleagues will be pleased with your success, even the nicest of them will go through their own periods of self-doubt and some amount of jealousy. Make it easy on them, not only because it's the nice thing to do, but because it further cements your relationship with an important group of people who will—at least *should*—become part of your continuing network. Vow to keep in touch, and be sure you do.

Another natural tendency of a departing employee is to coast through the final weeks of employment. While some of that is expected, it behooves you to continue to expend solid effort right up until your final day. If your job is going to be taken over by others in the department, be especially cooperative in helping them get a good grasp on it as quickly as possible. If the company hires someone to fill your position before you leave, do everything you can to help that individual slide into the job smoothly and efficiently. Also, make sure your boss understands that you'll always be available to answer questions that will help your successor do a good job. Your boss will certainly appreciate this and remember you for it.

Try to be of help in finding your replacement. If you

know people who would be perfect for your job, mention them to your boss and urge that they be considered. Not only does this take a burden off your boss's shoulders—as well as those of the personnel department—it places someone in that company who will view you with some level of appreciation, and who will become an extremely important person in your ongoing networking. Be honest if you play a role in finding your successor, however. I've seen instances where a departing employee deliberately looked for someone less qualified in order to look good in absentia, or created impossible qualifications in order to make the point that the company was losing a good man.

If you've been fired for any reason, or dismissed as part of a general pruning of staff, everything I've suggested a resigning employee should do is valid, too.

Obviously, it's much more difficult to leave under these circumstances. If it has resulted from an outright clash between you and your superiors, it's going to take a lot to keep bad feelings you harbor from surfacing. Still, I urge you to try. No matter why you've been asked to leave, you have nothing to gain, and even more to lose, by making a negative situation worse.

Being fired is a traumatic experience. We're flooded with feelings, most of them negative. Frustration, disappointment, anger, and guilt all compete within us at once. Don't react until you've had a few days to cool down and are able to view the situation with more clarity and reason. When you have reached this point (don't take too long) you should begin a systematic campaign to ease the ramifications of having lost your job.

First, plead for time. Because you've been told to vacate your office by the end of the week doesn't necessarily mean that has to be the case. Unless there is such rancor between you and the person who fired you that communication is impossible, sit down and calmly, rationally discuss your dismissal. *Ask* that you be given some additional time before leaving. The worst they can say is no. If you do manage to gain some time—and I've seen this happen on many occasions—you've extended your official employment, which, if you immediately get moving in search of another job, is a better position from which to look.

No matter what is churning inside you, try to keep all your communication on a positive level. Attempt to determine the sort of reference you'll be given. If it doesn't appear to be positive, try to change your boss's thinking about it. Ask for a written reference before you leave. Such references are often considered by a new employer as having been written under duress. Ask for it anyway. At least if you have a decent reference in writing, it might head off the potential of a former boss "leveling" with a reference seeker, even though what he or she says is, more often than not, ill founded and delivered in anger and pique.

Like an employee leaving for a better job, a dismissed employee sometimes is called upon to go through an exit interview. No matter how strong the temptation, no matter how much right you have on your side, try to get through it with as little complaining and finger-pointing as possible. Your goal from the moment you receive the pink slip is to smooth things out, soften the reasons for having been fired, and cut yourself the best possible deal under the circumstances. Do all your yelling and complaining to yourself in your car, or at home.

In an increasing number of companies, dismissed employees are offered the services of an outplacement counselor. These counselors come from firms that are retained by the company that's fired you, and are generally paid on a per-employee basis. It's always hard to determine how much altruism is involved in a company hiring such services. Certainly, some are sincerely interested in the well-being of a departing employee, and feel the expenditure of money to help that person get through the process of being fired and finding a new position is worth it in human terms.

On the other hand, it also represents good PR for the company. Fired employees who leave in anger express it to many people, including those in the company's industry. An employee who is sincerely helped by an outplacement service will leave with more positive feelings, especially if the counselor has materially helped the person get another job.

Sometimes a counselor from an outplacement firm is present, along with the boss, when an employee is brought in to be fired. I dislike this practice; it's like having a funeral director on hand at the hospital. If this happens to you, all you can do is try to make the best of it, again in an attempt to cut your losses.

Make an honest attempt to determine whether you really need the services of an outplacement counselor. Some people do, especially those who perceive themselves as having special problems, or who haven't planned for such an eventuality (haven't "insured" their careers on a continuous basis).

On the other hand, if you are someone who is confident you'll find another job fairly quickly, suggest to the company from which you're departing that you be paid additional severance roughly equaling the amount the company would pay to an outplacement service. Better to have that money in your checking account than in the coffers of the outplacement firm.

If you do elect to use the services of outplacement counseling, it doesn't mean you have to accept everything suggested to you. If you feel the counselor is not earning his or her money, by all means report it back to your former boss, or to the human resources department. After all, counselors are being paid good money to help you. If they don't, hopefully your former company will take steps to get you a more effective counselor. But make sure your evaluation is based upon reason and is not the result of lingering anger and a need for revenge.

What most people being fired don't realize is that there is room for negotiation. Too many simply pack up their belongings and slink out, head bowed, accepting only what they were given in their severance package. Ask for more severance pay if you honestly believe you deserve it. Negotiate the time you'll be allowed to use a desk at the company, its phone, its fax machine, photocopier, and secretarial services. These things can make a dramatic difference in how fast you'll locate a new job. To neglect to pursue them is to shortchange yourself.

The first thing that comes to many people's minds these days when fired is to threaten a lawsuit. Certainly there are instances in which legal action is called for, especially in cases of blatant discrimination based upon age, race, sex, and other human elements that are protected under our employment laws.

But in most cases someone is fired for "good" cause, and the discrimination excuse is merely contrived. My research indicates that most people who are fired knew they were going to be long before the ax actually fell. Companies these days, well aware of the penchant for suing former employers, do a pretty careful job of documenting an employee's slipping performance, bad attitude, and general lack of productivity. Bringing a frivolous lawsuit against a former employer based upon a need for revenge guarantees that you have burned your bridge back to that company and its potential contacts. You've completely destroyed the possibility of getting even a reasonably satisfactory reference.

How you leave a job can be vitally important in your search for a better one. Don't be shortsighted. View the company you're leaving, either because you've elected to leave or have been asked to, as but another steppingstone in your continuing search for career success. Commit yourself to leaving a job the right way, just as you have committed yourself to finding that better job.

Reminders on How to Leave a Job

≡ Keep your behavior on a professional level, no matter how angry you are.

≡ Be positive, both when informing your boss you're leaving and in your resignation letter. Make sure a copy of the letter goes to the company's personnel or human resources manager.

≡ Give a fair amount of notice.

≡ Be especially helpful to the person or persons replacing you.

≡ Don't gloat about your new job to present colleagues.

≡ Don't coast at the end. Give your final weeks your all.

≡ Try to come up with your own replacement.

≡ If fired, negotiate the best possible deal you can.

≡ If fired, try to get a written reference.

≡ Don't threaten to sue.

31 · THE IMPORTANCE OF A SENSE OF HUMOR

Don't let the joke be on you

A SURVEY I COMMISSIONED NOT LONG AGO HAD to do with sense of humor and its correlation to career success. We asked personnel directors and vice-presidents from a cross-section of America's largest corporations: "Do people with a sense of humor do better—the same as—or worse at their jobs than those people who have little or no sense of humor?"

Eighty-four percent replied that, in their opinion, employees with a sense of humor do a better job than those lacking that wonderful human quality. (Whether the remaining 16 percent lacked a sense of humor themselves must remain conjecture.)

Note should be made that the "popularity" of certain employees wasn't a factor in this study. The 84 percent made it clear that they felt that those employees with a sense of humor *did a better job*.

It isn't difficult to apply the results of that survey to anyone *seeking* a better job. Not only is a job candidate with a sense of humor more pleasant to interview (which means more likely to get the job), but humor—and the ability to smile easily—can have a measurable positive effect on every job seeker when going in for an interview.

Let's face it, a job interview evokes a level of tension and apprehension in every job candidate, the degree determined by how experienced he or she is at the process. The physical act of smiling relaxes people. I've noticed it myself when about to be interviewed on television. I'll see myself in a monitor and be aware that there is an expression on my face, especially my lips, that I don't like. It's a small thing, but there's a quality to it that indicates to the interviewer that I'm nervous. Every time this happens, I think of the word *smile*. That's all. I don't actually smile. I just think about it. And, without fail, my lips and face fall into a more relaxed, pleasant expression.

Using a sense of humor when looking for a job is tricky. Too many people try to be funny on their résumés and in their covering letters. That's a mistake; don't do it. A good sense of humor does not mean being an office clown or always cracking jokes. In fact, telling jokes in today's workplace can be risky. Some court rulings have held that telling off-color jokes in mixed company at the office can be construed as sexual harassment. Jokes that depend upon ethnic stereotypes are patently offensive to most people. No, jokes do not necessarily translate into a sense of humor.

I prefer to define a good sense of humor as appreciating the fact that life and people are never perfect. People with a genuine sense of humor are pleasant and easy to be with. These men and women are able to appreciate the foibles of the everyday workplace and can smile when the going gets tough. Tense, unpleasant situations are often defused by such people, and they are a joy to work with.

This doesn't represent a new philosophy. Cicero, who was around *long* before any of my surveys, said, "Joking and humor are pleasant and often of extreme utility."

A sense of humor—laughter—has other values besides helping you do a better job. The ability to laugh is therapeutic. A study at the University of California at Santa Barbara determined that "laughter is indeed a tonic. It stimulates the cardiovascular system and reduces hypertension, depression, heart attacks and strokes."

People with a sense of humor also seem to be sharper people. I recall a former Arizona congressman, Morris Udall, saying once, "Humor keeps my mind sharp." Udall was always considered one of the most genuinely humorous men in Congress.

People with a good sense of humor seem to have a greater appreciation of words. They're able to take two incongruous ideas and juxtapose them. They are able to look at a mundane situation, one that others are viewing with unnecessary horror or concern, and apply an irreverent interpretation to it. The end result is that such demanding situations become more manageable, and those charged with managing them find they're able to do it better and quicker.

Obviously, possessing a sense of humor in business situations, and not being afraid to exhibit it, doesn't mean turning serious business problems into laughing matters. But being able to smile when the pressure is on, and being able to see the less serious side of adversity, is a valuable attribute for any man or woman seeking a better job. Just being able to appreciate the soft, human, and humorous side of this crazy world can take you a long way.

The survey I mentioned at the beginning of this chapter didn't stop at asking whether a sense of humor helped people do a better job. We also asked who the respondents felt possessed "the best" sense of humor in business.

Thirty-two percent felt that top management had the best, while 28 percent gave that honor to middle managers. Eighteen percent voted for other staff personnel. This, of course, raises an interesting chicken-and-egg question. Are top managers more willing to display a sense of humor than lower-level staff people because they hold more secure and lofty positions, or did they get to those positions because they had a sense of humor to begin with?

Someone once said that business is no laughing matter. The intent of business is undoubtedly serious, but the day-to-day "business" of conducting business leaves plenty of room for humor. Take stock of your humor quotient, and be sure that you're approaching the demands of today's better jobs with a good one. The least you can do is be pleasant. It's easy to hire nice people—it's tough to hire someone you don't like.

If you haven't got a sense of humor in today's business world, the joke could end up being on you.

32 · BEING SERIOUS IN YOUR JOB SEARCH

Just browsing, thank you

WE ALL KNOW BROWSERS.

I know a couple who spend part of virtually every Saturday looking at new cars. They drive a 1982 Pontiac. Obviously, they don't intend to buy a new one, but enjoy the experience of looking at them.

There are house browsers, couples who devote literally hundreds of weekends over the course of years looking at houses, yet never buy.

People browse for many things. It represents a particular interest of theirs, a time-consuming, albeit pleasant hobby. Of course, the time they consume of others—like car salesmen and real estate agents—is another matter. I suppose these salespeople chalk up having to deal with browsers as coming with the territory.

There are browsers in the employment field, too. I've run across many of them in my years of dealing with job candidates. These employment browsers are constantly searching for a better job, but when better jobs are offered them, they always have reasons not to take them. I often get the feeling that these people are dealing from a definite lack of self-esteem, and must constantly affirm their desirability by being offered jobs. An analogy, I sup-

206

pose, is to a man or woman who flirts with a member of the opposite sex until being asked out. Being asked—being wanted—is enough, and they turn down the date.

Like the car and house browser, job browsers evidently enjoy the process of *looking* for a job, something I'll never understand. They send out countless résumés, are constantly sneaking off from their current employment to be interviewed, take calls from headhunters and encourage them to keep looking for them, but never react when an offer is made.

If you're one of these people, find another hobby. What happens in so many cases is that these job browsers send résumés to so many companies, and are interviewed by so many executives, that the word invariably gets back to their current employer that they're looking for another job. Result? Losing the good job they already have.

Interestingly enough, there are also "employer browsers." These are companies (more accurately, individual executives within the company) who are constantly looking for people without any intention of hiring. They keep interviewing, never offer a job to any of them, and quickly give the company the reputation that no one can make a decision there. At the same time, the word gets around that the company has a high turnover rate, which keeps really good people from applying there. And their present employees constantly feel their jobs are in jeopardy because Mr. Smith or Ms. Jones "is interviewing people again." They read this as meaning that the company is marking time until the perfect candidate comes through the door to replace them.

In either case, the practice is a bad one and should be avoided.

That doesn't mean, however, that you shouldn't occasionally go out and test the waters. We all need to do that from time to time, if only to establish our relative worth in the marketplace. And by poking your head out on occasion, you might discover that things are a lot better where you are currently than you thought, and you're better off staying put.

If you decide to test the employment waters now and then, do it on the basis that if something does come along that truly represents a better job, you'll seriously consider taking it.

33 · CHANGING SOCIAL MORES AND THE WORKPLACE

Things will never be the same

THERE IS NO PLACE IN OUR BUSINESS WORLD FOR social preferences when looking for a job. If you fail to heed and adopt that philosophy, you'll find yourself very much out of sync in today's world. In fact, you're likely to hold yourself back if you arbitrarily restrict the type of company or individuals for whom you'll work. Yes, it's perfectly legal for you, the job seeker, to discriminate because of race, color, creed, national origin, religion, age, handicaps, and sex. You don't have to accept a job with any company, or work for any individual for any reason whatsoever—except, perhaps, if you're collecting unemployment insurance.

But consider this. If you make such judgments where jobs are concerned, you may very well be taking a giant step backward in your search for success.

If you're a single man, you're one of approximately 24.4 million single males in America. If you're an unmarried woman, there are almost 34 million women in this country with the same marital status.

Two decades ago the number of people who never married made up about 16.2 percent of the adult population. Now that figure is placed at above 22 percent.

Similarly, only 3.2 percent of the adult population was divorced in 1970. That number is now well over 7 percent. (This includes *all* adults; as we know, the divorce rate for recent marriages is much higher.)

One of the major hallmarks of this changing world is represented by the above figures. As sexual mores and patterns of male-female living have evolved over the past forty years, business has had to change, too, in the way it views people and their private lives. This hasn't been easy for many managers, who were brought up in an era in which the roles of men and women were more clearly defined. It wasn't long ago that a married man stood a better chance of being hired than an unmarried man, even though the unmarried man's credentials might have been equal or even better. That's no longer true in most cases. As more and more new managers come out of the ranks of those who've lived their lives differently in this new age, their attitudes naturally will influence the way a person's marital status is perceived. That probably leaves some old-line managers basing many of their hiring decisions on such prejudices.

Married men were always perceived as bringing more stability to a company. They were thought to be less likely to carouse at night, and because they had significant family demands made upon them—especially financial—more likely to work harder and take their jobs more seriously. That preconditioned notion never seemed to apply to women, probably because women were not viewed as primary wage earners, but working only to supplement the family income.

The women's movement changed all that, and the uncertain economic situation within our society today has made it absolutely necessary for millions of women to seek employment.

More important—and this is what an increasing

number of male managers seem to be grasping—women are now seeking the same fulfillment from a successful career that men have always sought. Fortunately, they have been able to achieve this to an impressive extent considering how far they have had to come in a short period of time.

The labor department projects that twelve years from now more than 80 percent of *new* employees—not only new entrants into the work force—will be protected minorities and women. Not only does this translate into a huge pool of new people competing for the job you're going after, it will more drastically change the atmosphere of every company.

So what does this mean? It means that the white married man will have more competition from nonwhites, singles, the divorced, and, primarily, women. Men will have more competition for better jobs, and those who compete best will be those men who are constantly on the alert to improve options within their company, or with another.

It means that there will be more people—men and women, whites and nonwhites—all vying for better jobs. Fortunately, the growth of our nation, the emergence of new technologies, and the overall strength of the economy will create an increasing number of better jobs as the world becomes just a little bit less crazy.

34·DISCRIMINATION IN THE WORKPLACE

My boss is a woman, but she's pretty good

PEOPLE WHO MAKE COMMENTS LIKE THE ABOVE always give away their secret prejudices. We'll hear people say, "My neighbor is black, but he's a decent guy." Or the classic "Some of my best friends are..." (You fill in the blank.)

I mentioned in the previous chapter how American business has had to alter its perceptions based upon changes in society where men and women are concerned. That's certainly true to a great extent, but it doesn't necessarily extend to all women in the workplace. Yes, more women than ever before are not only being hired but being given top executive positions. That's the good news. The bad news is that every survey on the subject of salaries for men and women indicates that, in general, women are paid 35 percent less than men for doing the same job. I suppose this represents an advance of sorts; undoubtedly, the figure was even lower a few decades ago.

Perhaps the reason has to do with the fact that women have made their biggest impact on the workplace only in recent years, and the age level of employed women, on the average, is lower than for men.

At the same time, remember, as I said before, if you operate on the premise that you'll always have less responsible jobs at less pay because you're a woman or a member of a minority group, you may subconsciously turn that belief into reality. We do it in many areas of our working lives—give in to something over which we have little or no control, then become convinced that we have not succeeded because of *it*. Certainly, there are negative factors outside ourselves that have the potential to cause us problems, but, whether perceived or actual, it is our responsibility to recognize them and create ways to cope with them in order to convert them to our advantage, rather than go through life feeling victimized.

Many problems faced by women, as a group, in today's workplace are also problems for individuals of all types, male and female alike.

Take age as an example, which I've addressed specifically in other chapters. If someone considers him- or herself too old to land a better job, that attitude will be evident and will surely stymie the person's chances for success. On the other hand, if that same person views being somewhat older as something positive, a good share of opportunities for better jobs will be the result.

I've encountered a legion of job seekers in my career who operate under the handicap of what I call the "Too Syndrome." They explain away their failures by saying they're too short or too tall; too homely or too good-looking; have too little experience or too much; too little education or too much. And, in the case of some women, "The workplace is too prejudiced against women for me to really succeed."

Women who think this way when pursuing jobs, and going through interviews, assume that the male behind the desk doing the hiring considers women not to be career-oriented enough...or that women get married, have children, and don't return to work...or that women aren't tough enough to withstand big business's rough-and-tumble rat race...or that women are too sensitive.

The list goes on.

The best approach any woman with career aspirations can take is to counteract any such myths—if they exist at all with any given male interviewer—before they are allowed to influence a hiring decision. I recommend that women prepare, as part of their overall approach to an interview, *answers* to those myths and questions. They might well be on an interviewer's mind, but won't be asked because it is against the law of the land.

Such questions as "Is she married?", "Does she expect to get married?", "Is she living with someone?", "She's married; how soon does she plan to start a family?" might be answered without the questions being asked, if you think it's to your advantage and would help you nail down a job offer. For instance, here's something you might say during the interview, if you consider it appropriate:

"I think this position you're filling is a wonderful opportunity for me, and I assure you that if you hire me, you won't be sorry. My husband and I both have solid work ethics. He's a partner with a major CPA firm, and we own an apartment ten minutes from this office. We don't have any children, and we share household responsibilities beautifully. I consider myself someone who works equally well with men and women."

This approach holds true for anyone who anticipates prejudice that might be practiced against him or her, no matter how subtly. If you're older, project what questions might arise with the interviewer, and put his or her mind at rest up-front. If you think your age is holding you back, it will. Combat the problem during the interview by counteracting such prejudices. For example, you might inject into the interview something like: "Ms. Brown, I must tell you that I'm proud of my attendance record. In the last two years I was only out once, and that was for three days. I'm not only extremely accurate in the work I do, I pride myself on being able to complete a project in the least possible time in order to free myself up for new assignments. I guess what it amounts to is that I enjoy working and take a lot of pride in what results I'm able to achieve."

It's my sincere belief that competent women have better opportunities today than equally competent men. Men are just beginning to recognize that the effective number of qualified people vying for better jobs has at least doubled in the past twenty-five years. Men now know that they have 100 percent more competition than they used to have—women!

Ten years ago we did a survey that I found interesting, if not startling. We examined the files of job candidates we sent on interviews for financial middle-management positions. The survey revealed that when at least one woman was interviewed for the position—no matter how many men were interviewed for the same opening—women were hired in 73.3 percent of the cases.

When I started my career on the way to becoming a Certified Public Accountant, women were a rarity in public accounting. I worked with two women in a large CPA firm that employed mostly men. I must admit they were superior accountants. I rationalized that men and women were equal in innate ability, but that women tried that much harder in the man's world of accounting. Today, more than half of college accounting graduates are women, and women hold jobs of tremendous responsibility in all areas of finance and accounting.

There is absolutely no room for discrimination or prejudice in any area of hiring. I've always had a fetish about this subject, and have fought for equal rights throughout my many years in personnel recruiting. When I first started in 1948, some newspapers still accepted ads that were blatantly discriminatory—for example, "only Christians need apply." Age requirements were more frequent than not, and women were easily omitted from the better jobs in the classified section of major newspapers because the better jobs all appeared under the heading: "Help Wanted, Male." That's the way jobs were filled in those days, and I have to tell you I certainly wasn't very proud of it.

When I was president of our trade association in the early 1950s I wrote an article titled: "It's as Simple as Black and White." I pointed out to our members that the world has changed and will never be the same. Discrimination because of color has no more place in our society —it's not only inhumane, it's bad business to discriminate. I had some insight into the problems of blacks. I was a volunteer ambulance driver in the 1940s, one night a week from 7:00 P.M. to 7:00 A.M., for Sydenham Hospital in Harlem. I did this volunteer work for two years, and our group took the conventional police phone calls. Sydenham was experimenting at the time with a "revolutionary" plan of black doctors working alongside white doctors and black nurses working with white nurses. It didn't take me long to realize that, black or white, I should judge them on what I perceived was their ability. I found them the same—some of each group were good and some were not so good.

Prejudice of various kinds and strengths, against various groups, is still with us, and at times spills over into the hiring process when certain individuals are involved.

I know *this,* however: those individuals are far fewer than forty years ago. We've come a long way—thank God.

Whatever sex, religion, ethnic background, or color you are, you owe it to yourself to not allow those things to keep you from finding better jobs. They're out there for everyone, unless you go after them assuming you won't get them because you're too...

35·SHOULD YOU START YOUR OWN BUSINESS?

I think I'll go out and do my own thing

THE DRIVE FOR SELF-OWNERSHIP IS KEENER than ever. It is estimated that about 1.5 million new business ventures are created each year.

Starting one's own business has always been appealing, and is an integral part of the American fabric. Most American workers spend some time thinking about being their own boss and reaping the rewards of such enterprise. This fantasy becomes especially prevalent when you've lost your job or reached a point of dissatisfaction with your present one. When we're about to be between jobs, it's the natural time to wonder whether this is the moment we should strike out on our own.

Maybe it is.

Maybe it isn't.

Whenever I talk of "career insurance"—taking whatever steps are necessary to ensure your career—I advocate having strong interests outside of your full-time employment, interests that can be nurtured into a part-time source of income and, should you be without permanent work, can be quickly turned into a primary source. But that's different from striking out on your own without the support of a steady paycheck.

Let's look at both options—being totally on your own and moonlighting.

First, moonlighting.

Each person has his or her own reason for moonlighting. For many, it represents nothing more than additional income to supplement a regular salary that's being stretched thin. People in this category generally do not start their own businesses. Instead, they take a job on nights and weekends and, in general, are not looking to develop their after-hours activities into anything more than a set wage for hours worked.

A second category of moonlighters are those people who enjoy the psychological payoff of being in charge of a business venture, even though it may not provide significant additional income, or is not likely to be developed to the extent that it would one day replace the need to be employed.

The third category is represented by people who, while making a living by working for someone else, have dreams of building their personal creation into a viable enterprise that one day will prosper and will provide them with all the money and perks of entrepreneurial success. These men and women generally spend a great deal of their spare time developing such ventures.

Before I talk about each category, let me introduce some thoughts that apply to all three.

Employers have mixed reactions to employees who hold outside jobs. It depends entirely upon the perception of the boss. Some applaud the kind of initiative demonstrated by employees who go out and use their off-hours to make more money. For others, it represents a threat. These bosses are concerned that employees who either wish to or need to supplement their income are not paying sufficient attention to their primary jobs.

In either case, I've always recommended that employees who intended to moonlight inform their immediate boss of their intention and, in effect, seek their approval. Obviously, this is not necessary in many cases, particularly when lower-level employment is involved, but if you're in management, you might find that moonlighting on the sly could seriously hamper your advancement opportunities with your current employer.

The type of job you choose to moonlight on has bearing here. Working part time for a competitor will almost always guarantee your dismissal from your full-time job, and with good reason. A while back, I knew a highly experienced CPA with a major accounting firm who was discovered to be doing tax preparation on the side. The discovery was made during the height of the tax season, and no accounting firm wants to lose a valued and experienced staff member during this peak period. But this individual was fired on the spot.

Moonlighting is an American way of life. Just be sure you don't earn extra money at the expense of your major income.

If you decide to run your own small business on the side—probably out of your home—you're one of more than 25 million Americans in 19 million households whose office is their basement, spare bedroom, or diningroom table. Approximately 16 million are part-time home workers, and 9 million are running full-time businesses from a house or apartment. The total number increased about 40 percent between 1985 and 1988. It's estimated that by the year 2000 there will be more than 40 million Americans working from home.

Eight out of ten small businesses fail. The reason usually given is that there wasn't sufficient capital to sustain the business through the difficult start-up years. While that undoubtedly plays a role in the demise of many small businesses, my instincts tell me that a lack of business experience probably plays a greater one, especially in recent decades characterized by a need for instant gratification. How many failed businesses were started by men and women without sufficient experience and knowledge can't be measured. I suspect the percentage is high.

Working is a teaching experience in and of itself. Our first jobs, as menial as they might be, expose us to the business world and its demands. Unless we've absorbed sufficient information and knowledge through the process of working, we start our own businesses with built-in deficits that are potentially more damaging than a lack of start-up capital.

That's not to say that we shouldn't act upon our dreams of striking out on our own. America was built that way, and will continue to be. I do caution, however, that you view being on your own in the same way I urged you in chapter 9 to analyze whether the grass is truly greener at another company. Be certain that if you do leave a permanent job for your own business, you do it for positive reasons, not as an escape from what you consider an unpleasant and stifling full-time job. There are better ways to "escape" than jumping into the tricky entrepreneurial waters without a life jacket.

If you are determined to start your own business, first do it on the side. This means giving up leisure time. If the dream is compelling enough, you won't consider yourself deprived. Be sure you don't short-change your permanent employers by "stealing" their time, materials, and services. Apply the concepts of ethics, loyalty, and hard work to both endeavors.

Finally, if you go it alone because you don't like having a boss, remember that everyone has a boss, including the owners of any business. For them, the customer is the boss, and is more demanding than any person in a corporate chain of command.

36· ONCE YOU'VE LANDED YOUR BETTER JOB

So you got the job. Now what?

CONGRATULATIONS ARE IN ORDER. AFTER ALL the maneuvering, networking, résumés, cover letters, follow-up letters, and interviews, you managed to navigate in this crazy world and get yourself the better job you wanted. Good for you. I can hear you now: "Whew, it's over."

It isn't over, for two reasons.

First, if you're thinking that way, you may find yourself *having* to look for another job sooner than you anticipated. Beginning a new job throws you into a new challenge, an even bigger one than landing it in the first place.

Second, unless you're a rarity, even if you don't *need* to look for another job, chances are you will. As mentioned earlier, the market for gold retirement watches has decreased considerably.

The simple fact that you've been chosen over others, and have been hired, is not necessarily synonymous with *having* a better job for a long period of time. New employees are almost always evaluated on a probationary basis. It may not have been intended that way, but that's the real world. It might be a month, three months, six months; no matter what the length of time, that probationary period does exist, and if your new employers feel they have made a mistake, they won't hesitate to say, "Look, sorry, but it just didn't work out." Actually, that's better than being disappointed in you but letting you continue to work there. When that happens, your long-term potential is virtually nil, and unless you take the bull by the horns, recognize the situation, and start looking again, you'll stagnate in your new "better job."

This brings up a very important point. Chances are that during your search for a better job, you were interviewed by a number of companies. Even though you chose not to accept a job with them, or were turned down, you should write each of them a personalized letter thanking them, and indicating you hope your paths cross once again (you may need them sooner than you think). And by all means include their names in your ongoing network.

It doesn't matter what level of employment you're at. You're the new kid on the block, the new employee, the unknown quantity, and how you attack those early days will determine, to a great extent, how you fare in the near and distant future.

Every corporation, every company has its own "culture." It's run by individuals who bring to it their own particular style, personality, and views of how this business can best succeed. Of course, the industry in which it functions plays a role. Certain industries have established an "industrial culture," and successful companies within it generally follow suit. That isn't always the case, however. The computer industry was dominated by "Big Blue," IBM, which was known for imposing upon its executives a rather stringent dress code: dark suit, white shirt, muted tie. Then along came the computer hotshots who operated out of garages and wore jeans and sneakers and T-shirts. Apple Computer defined that style of management in its early days and, as we all know, has been an incredible success in what was a staid and conservative computer industry.

And, of course, there is the Japanese computer industry, with its own distinct culture bred on the general Japanese culture itself, whose presence can't be denied.

When you first walk into your new job, have your antennae up to maximum length. Be receptive; let your eyes and ears and other senses take everything in to be processed. Is it a first-name company, or more formal than that? How do people dress in your department and in the company as a whole? Do the executives with whom you work drop into each other's open offices for informal chats about business matters, or have you entered a memo mill where anything of substance is put in writing and talks with other executives are scheduled through secretaries? Be quick in sizing this up. How quickly and smoothly you adapt to your new corporate culture can make a big difference in how rapidly you'll advance in it.

That doesn't mean having to be "one of the boys" (or one of the "girls"). In fact, I urge new employees to plan a strategy that allows them to fit comfortably into the culture, yet places them just a notch above. This is especially true in dress, which I talked about in chapter 17. Fit the mold, only fit it slightly better, with a modicum more of style. Match yourself to those with whom you work directly, but keep an eye on those in higher positions of management. How do *they* dress? How do they interact? Fit in naturally with your colleagues and peers, but keep your eye on the wider sphere, too.

Politics is an integral part of any corporate culture. We tend to look upon politics in its governmental sense as dirty business, one in which questions are evaded, false charges are made, and a whole array of dirty deeds take place in the interest of winning. There might be an element of that kind of politics in the corporation in which you've found your better job, but I would urge you to not view all company politics as being that way. After all, politics in its purest sense is nothing more than getting someone to see your point of view and side with you. Politics in this definition is a necessary and beneficial part of every aspect of our lives. We practice it in our marriages, with our children, in our social organizations, and, of course, in business.

Be astute enough to size up where the power lies in your department and, perhaps, beyond. Who seems to most often assume a leadership role? Who is the person others turn to for advice? Why has that person achieved that position? Will that person be a survivor in a major shake-up? What traits does he or she possess and demonstrate that have created this "political leader" in the department? Don't be misled by what others say, although don't dismiss their evaluations, either. But make your own judgments based upon what *you* see and hear, what you perceive. Put it all together—your observations as well as the comments of others—and learn to function smoothly within the prevailing political system.

Speaking of listening to others, be tuned in to whatever grapevine or grapevines are at work in your immediate department and in the company. Like politics, the grapevine has fallen into disrepute, and it doesn't deserve that status. Research indicates that as much as 80 percent of information disseminated to employees comes through the grapevine, and is reasonably accurate. This is especially true when managers are astute enough to recognize that the grapevine is more than a gossip mill. It is a viable and valuable conduit through which important management messages can be transmitted. Pay attention to the grapevine and learn from it. If you're a reasonable

person, you'll be able to differentiate between pure idle
gossip that has little basis in fact and information that
actually reflects certain situations within the company.

Be nice. Nice people are usually the last to be fired
and among the first to be promoted. If niceness comes
naturally to you, that gives you a leg up. If a nice personality is not part of your natural makeup, find a way to
inject more of it into your daily life. Don't be deliberately
pleasant with those who can help you in the company,
and unpleasant to those you feel are not in a position to
do so. Be nice to *everyone*. You never know who will be in
a position to help you, or to give you information that
will turn out to be useful in your ongoing career. Pleasant, genuinely nice people turn routine job assignments,
and pressure-filled ones, into more palatable experiences.
People who are dealt with pleasantly generally respond in
kind and do a better job.

From an even more pragmatic perspective, put yourself in the position of an executive deciding whom to promote from within. If two people are generally equal in
professional capability, but one is nice and one is not, it
simply makes sense to promote the nice person, someone
with whom that executive is going to have to work closely
on a daily basis.

Up until now I've stressed attitudinal aspects of
starting a new and better job. Now let's turn to more
labor-intensive matters.

A new job is a time to expend maximum energy. It is
not time to arrive late and leave early. The impression
you make during your initial weeks on a new job will be
lasting ones. No matter what level of employment you
function at, be willing to take on those assignments that
others who have been there longer wish to avoid. This
doesn't mean being a "patsy." What it does mean is demonstrating to those with whom you'll be working a will-

ingness to do menial work to make sure a job gets done. Be part of the team. Every new employee must work into the organization—and onto the team.

A new job is a confusing time, and you need to put in the extra hours to make it less so. You're going to have to conform to your new company's style. Your own established work structure, office procedures, filing systems, and other working habits you've developed over the years may have to be modified.

Every new employee has to go slow. In my many years of experience in employing managerial and placement personnel at Robert Half International, those new employees who tried to change things too fast not only suffered individually but tended to disrupt the smooth flow of our business. If every new employee attempted to change tried-and-true methods to suit his or her whims and personal preferences, businesses would quickly be in chaos. In every organization, individual needs must necessarily take a back seat to established company procedures. Don't misunderstand: I, like many employers, have always been open to new ideas, and many of the best have come from my own staff. Once someone has been in a job for a while and has had an opportunity to see firsthand how things work, suggestions for varying certain procedures are welcome. By giving it some time, an employee also has the chance to see why certain procedures are in place and shouldn't be changed. Give yourself several months before suggesting improvements. Not only will your evaluation be more likely to have meaning, it will be more readily accepted by higher-ups.

Devote yourself to getting things done. Every company, every boss understands that a new employee will take a period of time to adjust and become truly functional. The quicker you begin accomplishing things, however, the quicker you will be recognized as the right person to have been hired. Again, those extra hours you put in will make a big difference. Yes, take the time to analyze a project, and don't jump in as a know-it-all. But it is better to attack a project and make mistakes than to linger an inordinate amount of time, waiting until you have "learned enough" to do things right. Do it! A finished product can be improved; you can't improve on something you haven't even started.

Understand that no boss is interested in hearing why something couldn't be done. Sure, there are always situations in which factors outside your control get in the way of completing a job. But unless those are legitimate and understood, keep your excuses to yourself and get on with it.

Make sure you effectively use what time you have in any given day. Be hard-nosed about it. If you're wasting too much time talking to colleagues, take what steps are necessary to correct it, without offending them. Be realistic in evaluating the time it will take to do projects to which you've been assigned. Better to be up front about how long something will take to complete than have to announce on the due date that it isn't done.

Where projects are concerned, get in the habit of keeping your immediate boss informed on progress. This doesn't mean burdening him or her with long, detailed reports at every step of the way. Send an occasional brief note or pass a quick comment during a meeting so that your boss is informed of progress. If you leave the boss in the dark and a major problem develops, he or she is in a tough position with the person to whom he or she reports. It's all part of the concept of teamwork that every successful department, and company, benefits from.

Much of what I've suggested about getting a good start on a new job boils down to being a good listener. Good listeners quickly learn things; bad listeners never learn. It takes effort to be a good listener. Some people are naturally good at it, but most aren't. You have to concentrate on what the other person is saying, not constantly be thinking of what you want to say next. It's the same principle behind having a good memory, remembering the names of people to whom you've been introduced. People who remember names concentrate on them when the introduction is made. They're good listeners. Few things are more important to success than being a good listener.

Approach your new and better job with the right attitude. A surprising number of people find a better job and then go into it with a negative viewpoint. They find something wrong about it almost immediately, and never give themselves a chance to enjoy the thing they worked so hard to achieve—a better job in this crazy world.

Now that you've found it, don't lose it.

37 · YOUR FUTURE

Insuring your career

VIRTUALLY EVERY TECHNIQUE FOR GETTING A better job I've suggested in this book can be summed up under the concept of "career insurance."

The idea of insuring your career is one I've written extensively on because I believe strongly in it. When I first started suggesting that men and women insure their careers, I often received strange looks in return. We are all comfortable with the idea of insurance for our houses, our health, our cars, and our lives, but is it possible to *buy* career insurance?

I say it is, and it is more important in this tumultuous day and age than ever before.

The premiums you have to pay to insure your career aren't expensive in terms of dollars and cents. Money does have to be spent on a decent wardrobe and maintaining it, on business, trade, and professional subscriptions, an answering machine, decent stationery, and on other tangible assets every job seeker and career achiever must possess. But the real cost is paid through your hard work.

The more extensive and up-to-date your network of contacts, the more job insurance you own.

If you've created the personal personnel file I've suggested, the amount of job insurance is even higher.

It takes extra effort to seek out and write for those publications that will give you greater visibility within your company and your industry, but it's worth it.

You might have had to pay a premium in frustration when you left a previous job under unpleasant circumstances but managed to choreograph your exit on a positive and professional plane. That was worth it, too.

Continuing your education will cost you both time and money, but the value of your job insurance portfolio continues to grow.

If you've taken the time and effort to learn to communicate better as a speaker and in writing, that adds to your coverage, too.

Most important, when looking to insure one's career, is viewing our working life not in terms of one job after another, or one job for a long period of time. Rather, the maximum amount of career insurance is obtained when men and women in this crazy world view their working lives as a continuous progression, a series of steps that have been carefully considered, prepared for, and taken, and have developed a firm grounding and understanding of the principles of getting better jobs and building a successful lifetime career.

At the same time, while these principles are being followed, the attitude we carry throughout our career has never been more important. Finding a better job takes more than just a good résumé, an appropriate suit, and the right education. That's why I've touched upon such subjects as ethics, loyalty, and etiquette in this book.

Better jobs are out there for you. Whether you find and land them will have little to do with external factors. There may be some conditions beyond your control, the sort of things that have turned this world slightly crazy—

foreign takeovers, leveraged buyouts, widespread illiteracy, shifting values of society, drought, floods, and "bad luck." They are to be challenged and conquered, not viewed as insurmountable obstacles to achieving what we wish to achieve.

The world has always been crazy, at least from the perspective of those living in it. I'm certain the great Grecian and Roman scholars said on occasion, "I don't know what's happening to the world today. It's gone crazy!"

What really happens is that the world becomes more complicated and the changes so profound that it's hard for any of us to keep up with it. Of course, we do, one way or the other, because we must. Those who cope best become most successful, and are better able to improve their current jobs, or to locate better ones elsewhere.

I wish you all the best in landing better jobs, making them even better through your own efforts, and, at the same time, doing what you can to make this world a little less crazy for all of us.

Index

up-to-date information
and, 72–73
writing skills and, 68
loyalty, 3–4, 6, 12, 14–19
blind ads and, 89–90
discretion and, 16
hard work and, 18
layoffs and, 18–19
middle ground of, 15
promotion and, 16–17
reminders, 19
luck, 45–52
odds and, 46
reminders, 51–52

M

M, 113
Maslow, Abraham, 34
Me Generation, 7–8, 18, 57
dream jobs for, 30–31
loyalty of, 15
mergers, 75–81
emotional problems of
employees after, 80
job losses and, 76–77
loyalty and, 79
Molloy, John, 121
moonlighting, 219–221
for additional income, 219
as entrepreneurial, 219,
220–221
hazards of, 220
psychological payoff of, 219

N

National Association of
Temporary Services, 95
*National Business
Employment Weekly*, 125

Nebel, Long John, 152
networking, 46, 63, 82–87,
107, 222
investigations and, 169
by older workers, 59
references through, 83–84
salary ranges through, 185
secondary type of, 85
up-to-date list for, 78, 230
newspapers, 85, 87–91
niceness, 226
Nissan, 70

O

outplacement counselors,
198–199

P

pay-equalizing trend, 2
peak experiences, 34
personal personnel files, 47,
128, 231
Personnel Journal, 101
placement counselors, 3
productivity, 70–71

R

recruiters, 91–93, 207
ethics of, 93
return-calls percentage
and, 15
specialized, 91–92
references, 49, 83–84,
131–133
briefing of, 132
after dismissals, 198
résumés discussed with,
132